FOREWORD BY CHAIRMAN OF SSAFA
Soldiers', Sailors' and Airmen's Families Association

Although I am not an Army wife (that is an impossibility!) I have, over the years, had the pleasure of meeting many Service wives. I have through these meetings grown to appreciate both their loyalty to their husbands in the somewhat unpredictable lives they lead and their splendid sense of humour.

Gumboots and Pearls is a splendid demonstration of this humour and ability to laugh at some of the lighter aspects of military life.

Catherine Jones and Annie Musgrove, as co-authors of the book are kindly donating a percentage of the cover price to SSAFA which, as a charity, is responsible for the welfare of all families both past and present from the three services.

Although the book is by two Army wives, Naval and RAF families will find much in it with which to sympathise and enjoy.

Not having been a member of the Land Forces myself and having read *Gumboots and Pearls* I can only say how very glad I am that I went to sea!

Admiral Sir Peter Herbert KCB OBE
Chairman SSAFA

D0542980

ANNIE JONES
GUMBOOTS
AND
PEARLS
the life of a wife of.....

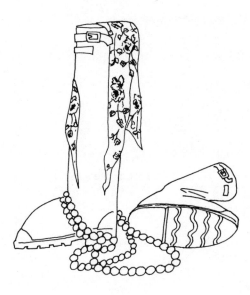

Illustrated by BOZ

First published August 1990
First reprint October 1990
Second reprint November 1990

Published by
OWL PRESS
PO Box 315, Kingston-Upon-Thames,
Surrey. KT2 5UL

Printed and bound in Great Britain by
SALISBURY PRINTING COMPANY LTD,
Salisbury, Wiltshire.

British Library Cataloguing in Publication Data
Jones, Annie
   Gumboots and pearls: the life of a wife of –
   I. Title
   829.91407

ISBN 0 9515917 0 3

OWL PRESS

CONTENTS

INTRODUCTION

The world is made up of all sorts of 'wives of'. There's the wife of the vicar, the doctor, the prep school master and even the tax inspector, and, of course the subject of this book, the wife of an Army Officer. All of them, but in particular Officers' wives, have the dubious privilege of marrying more than the man. It's quite unthinkable that they should want a career or life which is in anyway separate from their husbands'. They work as a team; husband and wife. They're the 'Jones' or the 'Williams' or the 'Wests'. The wife gives the coffee mornings and provides the back up service while her husband leads from the front; which makes the wife's role somewhat akin to that of the rear end of a pantomime cow. How many knew that they were letting themselves in for this when they opted for becoming a 'wife of'?

Of course not all Army wives are quite so naïve. Some of you knew precisely what you were doing when you got married. By the time you left home, Daddy was a Colonel and you had already moved house fifteen times. All that alien territory of duty coffee mornings and charity sales is your home ground.

There are also those of you who were already part of Army life. Nurses and teachers who, despite living in Army Messes, were remarkably free from Army lingo. It amazed you to discover that the Life Guard who lived down the corridor, was nothing to do with the local swimming pool but was legitimate quarry in the husband hunt. Your contribution to the Army as a wife is very valuable indeed. When, all too frequently, pompous officers make tedious speeches damning the morality of the youth of today, you may possess the secret knowledge of the birth mark on his right buttock. (Or was that another officer?)

'.... A LIFEGUARD ....'

But there are those of you who met your husband at university, or at a girlfriend's wedding. Besotted by the uniform, dazzled by the pomp and circumstance, you signed up for the duration; which in this case is a life time. Utterly clueless about the Army you quickly discovered that 'getting it wrong' can not only blight your husband's career but get you both posted to the Falkland Islands or Benbecula. The aim of this book is to help you avoid the pitfalls, so that you become a buoyancy aid rather than a sea anchor; you keep his promotion prospects afloat rather than be a drag on them.

A REGIMENTAL WEDDING

A CREDIT TO THE FAMILY?

When I told my mother I was marrying an Army
Officer she hit the roof, then the sherry bottle. If you
are not *born* into the Army this is the kind of response
you should expect. Civilians of my mother's
generation know what it will be like. Most of them
have been through it during National Service. Grotty
prefab housing, frozen loos through lack of heating
and endless separation from their husbands. They're
sure, after all the education and chances they've
given you, that you could have done better.

Questions of 'Where will you live?' 'How will you
ever get a job?' 'You won't be going abroad will you?'
will no doubt echo from wall to wall. For my part, I
was condemned as a failure. Marrying an Army
Officer certainly did not fulfill my parents'
expectations. (They'd hoped I'd be the next Prime
Minister). 'What about your degree?' they cried.
'After all we've done for you. Here you are with a
double first from Cambridge, a camp follower of the
British Army. What a waste!'

And so it happened. With a double first, in a subject
I can't remember, I was married into the Army to a

man called Nigel. (You'll find that there are quite a few Nigels in the Army. In my generation if they're not called Nigel, they're called Ian. Fads in names come and go. In ten years time all young Officers will probably be called Thomas, William or James.) For most people, growing up, getting married, and getting to know your husband is a gradual process of blunder and learning. Not so when marrying into the Army; undreamt of duties come thundering in overnight and you are expected to know what's what from the start.

GETTING IT 'RIGHT' FROM THE BEGINNING

Like it or not, you will be on parade on your wedding day. The other Officers' wives will be sizing you up. Get it wrong on your way to the altar and you have fallen at the first fence. The following guide lines may help you over a few hurdles.

You ought to have at least three bridesmaids and a couple of page boys. The page boys outfits don't matter too much. You can pick up presentable sailor suits at Laura Ashleys; they'll get them grubby in no time anyway. Handmade silk dresses are a must for the bridesmaids if they are to complement yours. Nothing too glamourous or you may find yourself outshone. A good designer will follow through your idea using your dress as a basis but without the hand sewn pearls. When thinking about your own dress you may find royal wedding dresses are useful as a starting point for ideas, but do remember they are designed for television and as such tend to be a bit on the vulgar side.

When dressing for your wedding a few points need to be borne in mind concerning the garter. Originally garters were a functional piece of underwear designed to hold up stockings. (Stockings themselves being very useful for hiding blotchy mosquito bites or for holding the cellulite together.) Wedding garters however, are quite different. Their role is to encourage stockings to be removed. The dilemma is whether wearing them will slow your man down or speed him up?

A further consideration is how high to wear them. A word of warning to you if you have never been near an Army wedding before. In some Regiments it is customary for a party of brother Officers to carry the bride. Their sole intention being to reveal your garter to the photographer's eye. If your thighs are best revealed only under cover of darkness then don't put your garter any higher than just above the knee.

In general, keep an eye on Royal Weddings. They are about as traditional as Army ones. You should certainly avoid changing the wedding lines like the plague; promising to obey your husband is fundamental to Army life. After all, Officers expect obedience from their dogs, so why should their wives be any different?

Get as many of your more presentable relatives to turn up as possible. Forget your trendy cousin from the LSE and stick to those who are guaranteed to wear morning dress or Aquascutum suits with pre-war hats. As his side will be knee-deep in khaki, it would show willing to drag out any relatives on your side who have been in the Services. The odd Brigadier or Naval Captain always go down well, and can bore the pants of his relatives at the reception. Remind old campaigners that medals are not to be worn.

The question of dogs is a bit tricky. All Officers have dogs and are rarely separated from them. They sit under their desks at work, are taken for runs and are generally kept to hand. Understanding padres may let them in, but on the whole you should request on the invitation that dogs are to be left outside. This gives the more devoted Officers a chance to regret their invitation before they have to be forcibly parted from Fido.

The groom will bribe all his fellow Officers to turn up in Blues (dress uniform) with the promise of a memorable booze up the night before. Getting into their Blues is an achievement in itself as they were measured for their uniforms when they were sprightly young things at Sandhurst. The more corpulent Officers may need a good deal of pushing and shoving (and half a pound of axle grease) to get into them. There's no need for alarm, they're quite used to wearing their uniforms like corsets. They're like that all the time at work. Hunting for buttons which have pinged off their jackets comes second only to searching for contact lenses as a time wasting pursuit.

For the Officers, dressing for the wedding is really a continuation of the booze up the night before. Hangovers are anaesthetised with champagne. The communal changing room atmosphere has its own charm, reminiscent of public school and the rugger pitch. Your husband will always be telling you how much the comradeship of the Army means to him. And you'll always be feeding those comrades who turn up unexpectedly at 10.30 p.m. on a Saturday night.

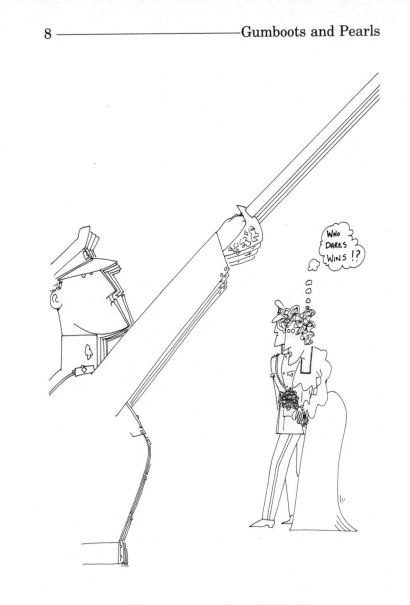

'KEEP YOUR HEAD ON THE SWORD WALK'

After the ceremony you are expected to walk under the swords. This is when the sobriety of the brother Officers is really critical. With swords held high they make a tunnel for you and your husband. You may have been married in church but marriage into the Army depends upon you walking under the swords. Remember to keep your head high, keep smiling and don't flinch if one of them sways. The origin of this ceremony is unknown to me, but clearly it makes a jolly spectacle and leaves your neighbours in no doubts as to your new position.

Engage a really professional photographer. If he is any good he will be able to keep the guests waiting for at least an hour for the group photograph. He will want you to act a re-run of the wedding, kiss your husband at the altar and look adoringly at your new acquisition. Be warned, rain or shine you will have to perform in front of a live audience. A really good photographer will send the guests outside whatever the weather.

If the wedding is held in the summer don't leave it too long before cutting the cake. On one memorable occasion the hot sun melted the icing and before the bride and groom could get to it, the whole thing toppled slowly sideways. It was shortly followed by the best man who was suffering from heat exhaustion.

Lastly, do remember the exuberance of the subalterns. Should you be foolish enough to divulge the name of your honeymoon hotel, you may find a reception committee you hadn't bargained for waiting to surprise you in your room.

THE HONEYMOON IS OVER

You may think that the glamourous life you led whilst being wooed is now yours for keeps. Wrong.... unless your husband has a substantial private income. In the single state Army Officers can afford to run MGs up and down to London, use a decent tailor and keep a couple of dogs. An attractive life-style to which you could very easily become accustomed. But once married, he will always be broke. Broke when you ask for a charge card at Harrods. Broke when you want your own MG. Most certainly broke when you ask for a cleaner. So be warned.

Many Army wives have been seduced by the idea of marrying a man in uniform rather than the man himself. After all an Army wedding is as good as a Royal Wedding when it comes to tradition and pageantry. (Well, almost.) But remember that when you get married, you won't just be marrying the man, Nigel, Ian or whatever, you'll be marrying the Army. Only very naïve wives think that they can get away without taking on the full role of an Officer's wife. Like a vicar's wife you'll be expected to open your house and ears to everyone and everything concerned with your husband's job. While most women in the twentieth century juggle the demands of a career and children, you will have a duty to support your husband thrown into the act as well. Under these circumstances you will find it easier to conform and abandon all thoughts of a career; you will be moving every year or so anyway. It makes more sense to forget you are living in the twentieth century, concentrate on your duties and have lots of children.

Officers' wives born and bred to it, know this when

they get married or even before. This saves them the
trial of staying at school after they are sixteen. They
can concentrate on getting a really good education in
things that matter like cordon bleu cookery and
deportment. When they get married they will
already have frilled blouses, pearls and twee little
baskets for doing the shopping. You can learn a lot
from Army wives like this who have been finished
properly. They will tell you that there is no room for
individuality. They know that the British Army is
the most traditional institution in the western
hemisphere, if not the world. (The Gurkhas come a
close second. But then we taught them everything
they know.) Watch a Liberal Party political
broadcast, even by accident, and you will be branded
as a communist for ever. Show too much leg at a
Ladies dinner night and you will be cornered in the
ladies loo by your husband's senior Officer's wife and
advised about dress. Like queues on benefit day at
the Post Office, surrender to the Army codes is
inevitable.

Sadly, every year there are a few casualties of
wives who wear themselves out kicking and
screaming at the System. Standard Army procedure
is for your husband's senior Officer to tell him to
'wind her neck in, old boy' and bring you to heel. Any
protests from you will undoubtedly draw predictable
comments from him, such as 'If you can't stand the
heat, get out of the kitchen' or 'If you can't take a joke
you shouldn't have joined.'

After a few years of futile battles most wives give in
and go in for more token gestures of rebellion, like
wearing red stockings.

If it's any compensation, the Army is a feudal
society. By marrying an Officer your position in the
ruling class is assured.

There are still a few whirlwind romances in the Army. You know the sort of thing, they meet over dinner, get married the next day and he's off on exercise the following week. Apart from the Falklands Campaign when this sort of thing was rife, most couples get on first name terms before they get married.

SEX AND THE ARMY OFFICER

Most Army Officers will have had some previous experience of sex, or at least say they have. At the very least they will have watched a bubble bath performance in Berlin or Hamburg while on Rest and Recuperation after an exercise. Some brother Officers may claim that your husband has had more intimate experience in the nightclubs of their youth. Such claims are to be dismissed. Single Officers usually drink too much to know who went with whom anyway.

Most Army wives are innocents by comparison. A few words of warning may help you avoid the worst of sex with an Army Officer.

1. Army Officers get dressed up like puffed up cockerels for Mess Dinners. They wear very tight trousers and metal spurs on their heels. Presumably these are a legacy from when they went everywhere on horseback – even to dinner. Most dinner nights in the Mess are men only affairs. Officers get drunk and in the absence of talking about women, politics and religion they tell a lot of war stories and dirty jokes. When your husband staggers in ratted and randy it's worth helping him take off his spurs before he gets

into bed or they'll rip your sheets and could hinder his performance.

2. Dogs. This is a tricky one. Your husband will be used to them sleeping by his bed in the Mess. If you can't stand an audience for your sex-life, it's worth insisting that they sleep in the kitchen. He may be a bit moody for a few weeks but you could always suggest he spends more time with them; taking them for walks, feeding them and possibly buying their food. If all else fails, he could sleep in the kitchen too.

'NEW TRICKS FOR AN OLD DOG?'

3. On no account apologise for not looking your best. Comments from you like, 'I'm sorry darling, I haven't had time to wash my hair' or 'I've got a dreadful runny nose' and such like, will draw corny barrack

room retorts like 'You don't look at the mantlepiece when you are stoking the fire.' Clearly something to be avoided at all costs.

4. If you are going out to a dinner make sure you bathe and dress with half an hour to spare. Most husbands can't resist a quickie with their wives at 6.30 in the evening. If you can't face the hassle of fending him off, get ready at the last minute when he's finished tying his bow tie.

When assessing your sex-life it's worth remembering that most Army Officers have had a very sheltered upbringing. On the whole they have lived from the age of six solely in the company of boys, men and dogs. This could explain a lot about his fantasies and grasp of the Facts of Life.

A WORD TO HUSBANDS

Now that you have fallen from the enviable position of a single Officer you may already miss the unquestioning servitude of the Mess servants. For those of you wondering how to get the best from your wife, here are a few tips.

1. Never give your wife any jobs to do first thing in the morning when she has all day to do them.

2. When explaining what is to be done, ensure that you are hidden behind the newspaper and mumbling with a mouthful of toast, or rushing out of the front door. That way, if you change your mind halfway through the day or discover you've given her the wrong information, you can blame her for not listening properly.

3. Never give your wife the correct instructions, telephone numbers or addresses. Hunting along high streets and phoning Directory Enquiries when you have gone will help keep you wife on her toes.

4. The best time to ask for lost wallets, keys, glasses and so on is when she is sitting down with a cup of tea. This will maintain her metabolic rate and prevent laziness from setting in. Make sure she is kept running up and down stairs as this will keep the cellulite off her thighs and prevent her from asking for an exercise bicycle or some such rubbish.

5. Do not promise to do anything, come home at a certain time or take her out. This will ensure that she continues to work hard to earn your approval and possibly some affection.

These are just a few ideas for you to work on. With regular training and practice your wife should gradually improve and may eventually become almost as good as the bat man you always wished you had.

SETTLING IN

QUARTERS

Now that you have married into the Army, you must learn not to refer to your new house as 'home' but as 'my quarter'. I have no idea what the origin of the word 'quarter' is. The dictionary gives me the definitions which I already know. To the Army a quarter is a lodging. To civilians a quarter is 'a fourth part'. To someone who inhabits a quarter the only connection between the two definitions is that the amount spent on the maintenance of one is a quarter of the amount required.

It is a regrettable fact, but many Army quarters are in a sorry state of repair. Like everywhere else there is a shortage of cash and nowhere is it more obvious than on the patch. So I must offer a word of advice to anyone who has not yet experienced the joys of living in an Army house. Don't judge the book by its cover – it's going to be far worse on the inside.

Long before you get to your new house you will have a rough idea of its age. If nothing else, it does prepare you for what is to come. Like looking at a horse's teeth, you can accurately judge the age of a quarter by looking at the address. Beware Balaclava Road and Khartoum Crescent – they probably rate as archaeological sites. Ypres Avenue and Somme Street should be avoided but you are getting onto fairly safe ground once you see Dunkirk Row or

Mulberry Way. I see Goose Green is cropping up now; isn't it nice to see traditions carrying on?

You may be extraordinarily lucky and move into a newly painted and refurbished quarter. However you are more likely to find that your quarter is next on the list for this treatment *when you move out*. But despite the paintwork and the state of repair, you can be sure that the inhabitants do everything in their power to make their current house as attractive as possible. In the same way that council house tenants who have 'bought' like to personalise their house with a neo-Georgian door or stick-on Cotswold stone, so Officers' wives like to ensure that people know their real status by festooning the place with hanging baskets and designer curtains. Unfortunately, there isn't much else you can do to disguise it. Although not all Army quarters are identical, it does seem as though there was a serious attempt to save money on architects' fees when they were originally built. (Don't think that I am suggesting that architects were not employed at all – although if you have had anything to do with Service housing you might have already formed that opinion.) No, the saving was made by only having half a dozen styles of houses designed. These have since been scattered throughout the Garrisons, both at home and overseas, so that patches are instantly recognisable to the cognoscenti. This is very handy when arriving at a new posting because you are easily able to find your new house. Mistakes do occur though if the Officers' patch is located near the local council estate, but the new arrivals usually realise pretty quickly that the state of repair of the latter is too good, and hunt around for something more dilapidated.

For those who are outside the Army system I should perhaps explain that all Army quarters are furnished with G-plan, unless you ask for it to be left empty. (Some people refer to it as F-plan because it makes you want to go...) This furniture was designed in the sixties and looks like it. Suffice it to say that until recently the covers for the three piece suite were psychedelic swirls in colour combinations of purple and turquoise or pink and orange. One can only assume that the Services master-minded a plan to get everyone to buy their own furniture by providing only stuff that would be universally loathed – and they almost succeeded. Since then it seems as though they have changed their minds, possibly because they felt they were going to get lynched by the wives. The covers are better now, but life must be proving too quiet for them; now that no-one is complaining, the covers are being changed again.

With these ubiquitous covers and walls universally painted magnolia, you know precisely what your new house will be like on the inside just by looking at the front door. You may be able to exercise a streak of originality with the arrangement of the furniture. This is often nipped in the bud as the rooms are so small that there is only one possible combination. Where larger rooms allow the imagination to flower, wives with a special talent get miffed when they discover that their good ideas have been pinched by everyone else. This particularly applies to the 'G-plan bureau'. This is a monstrous piece of furniture; a wooden Chimera, part desk, part bookcase, part sideboard and about as popular as the Greek monster of that name. It is a real problem. No one ever knows quite what to do with it. (Several suggestions have been made with regard to it and its designer, which have all proved to be physiological impossibilities.) However, should some bright spark discover a niche in her quarter into which it can be shoe-horned, you can be sure that every other one on the patch has migrated to the same spot inside a week. Plagiarism is a wonderful thing.

Because of the delights of Army furniture, some folk have given in and resorted to buying their own. Most people usually start off by just acquiring a few things, rather than a whole houseful straight away. Normally it's the three piece suite or the beds which people replace. The three piece suite because of the terrible issue covers, and the beds to get away from the integral bedside table. For those of you who have never met with this it is a seemingly good idea; one's first impression is that having the bedside table (in reality it is a small shelf with a drawer underneath) joined to the headboard is quite innocuous. Then you discover that you are unable to arrange the furniture in the bedroom how you would wish because now that the headboard is six feet wide the bed will only fit in one way. After that comes the realisation that it can ruin your sex-life. How? Easy, everytime things start to get interesting the sympathetic vibrations transmitted from the bed springs, through the headboard to the table cause the lamp to fall off at the critical moment. After this has happened for the third time you plan ahead and put the lamp on the floor before things get fruity. Safe in the knowledge that you will not be interrupted by an untimely crash you allow yourself to indulge in a little passion; then the drawer falls out. The next day your husband orders a new bed.

It is said amongst Army wives that you can always tell when some really major work is going to be carried out on your quarter because contractors appear to redecorate it. Once the house is spick and span you can be sure that within a fortnight a note will drop through the letter-box telling you that you are about to have replacement windows, or new wiring. Naturally when that has been done and you ask if the paintwork can be made good, you can be sure that the answer will be that the house isn't due to be done for another five years.

Unless you are unfortunate enough to live in a 'town-house', the Army euphemism for a flat, you will always get a garden. I use the term 'garden' loosely because it will probably consist of a mothy patch of grass and a chain-link fence to stop your kids from molesting the neighbour's cat. You may be fortunate and get something much bigger and more exciting than this but do remember the drawbacks. For a start, even if you have half an acre of lawn and an eight foot high hedge to surround it, you will still only be issued with a push mower and a pair of shears to keep it all under control. Try complaining and you will be helpfully told to 'try oiling the shears'. Having decided that the task is too much and invested in a motor mower and a hedge trimmer you can be certain that your next house will be blessed only with a balcony. Not much call for the motorised kit there unless you take to growing tryffids.

In Germany things are somewhat different. The houses are all rented from Germans and are built to their exacting standards. You will be certain of an attic, a cellar and a kitchen that is not only modern but spacious. Naturally it can't all be roses; you've got to live in Germany to get one (a subject I will enlarge on later). Still, everything else is recognisable; the furniture, the decor, the colour of the carpet so you are unlikely to feel homesick.

THE ART OF BECOMING A 'PAD' ON THE PATCH

Now that you have settled into your new home, you must start to get to know your neighbours and to join in with patch life. In order to be a really good 'pad' you should enjoy passing the time of day with the other wives. The maintenance of Army houses and their roads is always a good talking point. As you comment on the fatal looking potholes in the pavement a neighbour is bound to tell you that they resurfaced the perfectly serviceable road at least twice last year. 'Pads', that is residents on patches, always take an interest in the patch, if only to join in coffee and dinner party conversation.

There will always be some activity, heating systems being taken out or being put back in again, windows being replaced, paintwork painted, gutters being taken down and so on and on and on. When the contractors have finished painting your windows you can get the local maintenance man to chisel them open again. You can then get him to come back and insulate the gaps in your window frames and if you're lucky he'll come back again to touch up the paintwork. Pads, particularly Officers' wives come to enjoy this charade and include vast quantities of tea and biscuits in their weekly shopping.

Once you've been married for a few years and lived on a couple of patches you'll have no difficulty at all in settling down to being a true pad. Real pads talk about their neighbours they've known for two days as if they are life long friends. Then forget them just as quickly when they move out and a new lot move in. They invite neighbours for drinkies at Sunday lunchtime and can always be relied upon to feed cats and water plants when you are away, walk the dogs and have a good supply of tonic water in case you run out. As patch life hardly ever gets into the national press, real pads rarely leave the patch, even for a holiday, in case they miss out on something.

Becoming a pad is a simple process of narrowing your horizons and expectations. Remarks from your mother like, 'Darling. How on earth can you bear to live like this? It's like a council estate,' are to be expected. Remember that whatever your patch may look like from the outside it's who lives there that counts. You have the privilege of living with people of your rank and status and you don't have to mix with the riff-raff of civilian life. There are however a few things to remember when becoming a pad.

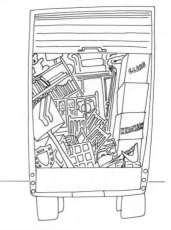

'ALL THAT FOR A SIX MONTH TOUR?'

Settling into patch life should be done as quickly as possible, after all you'll be lucky if you're there for more than two years. Most Officers' wives will do their utmost to welcome you. Their curiosity is always aroused by the sight of a removals van.

They'll all want to know how you've squeezed a full van load into an Army house. By the time they've seen the removals men carrying your collection of chamber pots and his collection of hunting trophies into the house, they'll be queueing up to invite you round for cups of coffee and, better still, strong gin and tonics to 'help with the move'. By the following morning everyone on the patch will know who you are, where you've come from and how long you're staying. The 'grapevine' has many tentacles. You will probably have visits from the rest of the patch wives and a few senior Officers' wives carrying pot plants by lunchtime.

There are always a few wives who aren't in the least bit interested in you. This is to be expected. They're probably moving themselves in the next few weeks to their new posting.

When you start to get to know your patch neighbours it is best to be rather circumspect about your domestic arrangements. Don't mention to anyone that you have a tumble drier, dishwasher, cleaning lady and a lady who does the ironing. Other wives will quickly resent this and will rarely invite you to their homes in case they are not as tidy as yours.

After a week or so, when you've had a chance to unpack and settle in, you should expect your new neighbours to be popping round. This is what living in a tight knit community is all about. When they call on you asking to borrow a cup of sugar or something, don't keep them on the doorstep. They'll be disappointed if they haven't had a good look round. Anyway, they'll probably invite you to lunch or coffee if you let them in.

Not all patches are the same. Some patches are deathly quiet. These are usually inhabited by older

Officers and their families. They've had the good sense to pack their children off to boarding school and can enjoy quiet term times with their dogs and the Times crossword. There are, however, patches dominated by younger Officers and their families. These are usually overrun by small children and dogs with far too much energy. It's never worth complaining about the noise your neighbours make. They're probably moving in a few months and he might turn out to be your husband's new boss. If you do start complaining, remember that Army beds are exceedingly creaky and they could have some legitimate complaints to make too.

After a couple of months of living in your quarter you will have run into all kinds of problems. Leaking tanks, radiators, broken down boilers are to be expected and a quick phone call to your estate warden is all that is needed. They're used to this kind of thing and usually send round their handyman to tinker with the boiler, radiator or whatever within a week.

If you're unfortunate enough to live in a quarter that has been left empty for a while you may find that there are more difficult structural problems to deal with. Even if you have mould growing down your bathroom wall on no account should you do any do-it-yourself maintenance on your house. The Army is always looking for the least excuse to cut down on their maintenance contracts. Before you know it, responsibility for quarters will be given to the pads. A horrendous thought and such a waste of time. Time that could be usefully spent holding lunch parties for senior Officers' wives. It's far better to hang pretty baskets of flowers over any structural and damp problems both inside and out. The Army will see to them in its own good time.

MESS LIFE

THE OFFICERS' MESS

The Officers' Mess is where single and separated married Officers live. The latter are generally referred to as bean stealers. This doesn't mean that they have a passion for healthy eating but prefer to live away from their families. This way they enjoy the servitude of the Mess Staff, four unbroken nights away from screaming children, a wife who is eager to see them at weekends and an excuse for a decent car. On top of all that they get cheap food and accommodation and they can sleep with their dogs.

Most Messes are the envy of the local civilians. While they hold dinner dances in church halls or pay for the privilege in hotels, Army Officers and their wives can use the Mess. If you should ever meet any civilians and hear them whingeing on about this there's no need whatsoever to feel guilty. Remember, being an Officer's wife you are part of the ruling class, not just in the Army but in society generally.

Undoubtedly some Messes are gems of our British heritage dating back to the sixteenth century. Unlike historic houses there is no shortage of government money to restore and maintain them. On the pretext of peacekeeping, Tory governments have increased the defence budget and wisely the Army has spent it on its Officers' accommodation. Officers' Messes need never be turned over to civilians. Rank does have its reward.

Not all Officers' Messes are of this pedigree. They can be roughly classified on the basis of age, furnishings, facilities such as croquet lawns and rules concerning women. On the whole a rough picture emerges and the most traditional and luxuriant Messes are used by the Cavalry and Guards who commute between the Mess and their club, while the red brick, austere monstrosities belong to the Corps.

GUARDS, CAVALRY AND INFANTRY MESSES

These are always ancient listed buildings. They're usually stuffed full of antique furniture which is constantly abused by the Officers. Regimental silver is everywhere, mostly acquired from India and other foreign parts when the word Empire wasn't just the name of the local cinema. Oil paintings and statues abound. Most have been shot up (literally) by the young Officers at Regimental dinner nights. The Mess oozes with the rich smell of furniture polish mingled with the smell of dogs. There are at least two croquet lawns. Mess staff can be relied on to polish the balls although Officers are expected to bring their own mallets.

Unlike dogs, ladies are not welcome in the Mess. Should you visit the Mess by accident you will be led to a ladies room to wait until you can be dealt with. Possibly once a year a Ladies dinner night will be held when wives are invited. Be warned, powder room facilities are pretty basic.

The Mess can be relied upon to take Horse and

'THERE'S SOME CHAP HERE FROM THE LOCAL INDIAN COMMUNITY GROUP.
HE SAYS CAN HE HAVE HIS PRICELESS ANTIQUES BACK ...
NOT TO MENTION HIS UNCLE!'

Hound, to choose their livestock, Country Life, to
choose their homes and the Tatler to choose their
wives (in that order of importance). Papers are
strictly limited to the Times and the Telegraph. Only
the Court and Social column gets read anyway.

CORPS MESSES

These red bricks of the Mess world range from late Victorian monstrosities to the post- war creations of the 1950s. On the whole these Messes have been furnished by the Army. Current stockpiles of G-Plan furniture will ensure that they continue to look the same through the twenty-first century if not the twenty-second. Recent redecoration of Messes has ensured that they are all colour co-ordinated. Frequently their red velvet curtains and red beer-resistant carpets make them look like a steak and chips pub. Silver is not much in evidence. The Corps reached India too late.

To make up for the absence of stables and croquet lawns the Corps Messes often organise things called Games Nights. Presumably these are to remind their members how glamourous their lives are compared to civilians. Ladies are invited and should wear evening dress while all the men wear black tie. Everyone gets frightfully excited about where the lumps are in the carpet during the highlight of the evening... indoor bowls.

Corps Messes take a variety of papers. These include the Times, Telegraph (of course), News of the World and the Sun. Never the Guardian with its ideology tantamount to treason. You probably still find copies of Country Life read by the dreamers. Copies of Motor Magazine and the Exchange and Mart are usually so well thumbed that they can't be read anyway.

GARRISON MESSES

These are the equivalent to cheap hotels. Some are still pre-fabs. The MOD must still be making a decision as to whether they are needed or not. Garrisons and their Messes exist throughout the United Kingdom and in the outposts of British influence which amazingly includes West Germany. These Messes serve all the Officers who haven't got their own (superior) Mess to go to. The only exception is the Garrison Commander. He is in charge of the Garrison and must use the Mess. Or at least be seen to.

Curry lunches are the backbone of Mess life on a Garrison. It's here that the Garrison Commander can meet the Medical Officer, the Military Police, the District Works Officer, the Padre and the WRACs. Civilians with so-called Officer status, who work in the Garrison, turn up without fail. Curry lunches are their perk. They usually all sit together on one table so there's no need for you to mix. For the Officer's wife Garrison society is a bit small and very definitely cliquey. Curry lunches are a must for catching up on the gossip from Saturday night's dinner parties. It's also a good opportunity for showing everyone how well the children behave. (If the children are revolting you can always show everyone how firm you are by taking young James or Camilla outside for a quick wallop.)

Garrison Messes have abandoned taking papers. The last time they took 'Women's Own' it was pinched.

KHAKI CATERING

When you are allowed to first set foot in an Officers' Mess you will discover the joys of Mess Catering. If you are a real Officer's Wife, born and bred to it, then you probably first tasted Army food at your christening because Mummy found it convenient to

use Daddy's Mess for the occasion. Having been
weaned on the stuff, you accept Army food without
question. For those who first meet the delights of the
Army Catering Corps (and I don't mean the chefs) at
their wedding reception it may take a little longer to
come to terms with it. For a start, the Army is
obviously worried about the heart condition of its
Officers. This is manifested, not by a low fat,
sugar-free diet, but by the lack of any element of
surprise in any of the fare they produce. Like drill
movements on the Parade Square, certain dishes are
dutifully marched out on certain occasions. Since the
Army loves tradition this doesn't bother anyone; in
fact woe betide those who try to introduce
new-fangled, wishy-washy ideas like cold desserts
instead of steamed pudding and custard. You must
not get the impression that it is the cooks that force
this fare on the Officers; it is, in fact, quite the
reverse. The chefs would love to try their hand at
charlotte russe or bavarois but the Officers, after
years of nannies and public school can't cope with
change and demand spotted dick.

As a wife you will only be allowed to encounter
Army catering at certain functions. Broadly
speaking these fall into four categories; the cocktail
party, the dinner night, the curry lunch and the ball.
You might be lucky and get invited to something else,
a luncheon party for a visiting royal perhaps, but you
will probably find that the food will fall into one or
other of these categories.

At the cocktail party you will first encounter the
'issue canapé'. These are much more ambitious than
anything you would produce and are designed as a
test to see who can cope with eating them. You would
be well advised to stick to the little biscuits with a
dollop of caviare as anyone can manage these without

embarrassment. The meat-balls-with-dip will leave you with the tricky problem of what to do with the sticks and anything in a puff-pastry case should be avoided like the plague. Whilst coping with the food you are expected to drink gin and tonic and keep up an animated conversation with a load of boring people. These are usually local civilians who have been invited along to try and stop them complaining the next time the Army inadvertently drops a live shell in their back garden. I suspect that cocktail party food is always the same in the hope that it doesn't upstage the guests – unfortunately, especially overseas, it often does.

Two or three times a year you will be invited to a Ladies dinner night. This is one of the few times you will be allowed out with your husband in his Mess Kit. Ladies dinner nights are fairly glamourous affairs, there will be a band, candles, the Mess silver and the food, for a certainty, will be:

Smoked Scotch Salmon

****

Beef Wellington (Boot)

****

Assorted vegetables

****

Pear Belle Helene

Your consolation is that the wine will be good and your husband will get value for money by getting totally drunk.

The high point of every Officers Mess social year is the Summer Ball. The first time you attend you will

be stunned by the fabulous selection of salads,
dressed sides of ham, dressed salmon, dressed turkey,
dressed anything........ In fact the only things which
aren't dressed are usually the wives who take this
opportunity to trot out the topless-evening-strap.
You will meet a similar cold collation at the
Sergeants' Mess Christmas Draw and at any
subsequent weddings. At each occasion you will
become increasingly amazed that so much food can be
covered in so much aspic for so little purpose.

Lastly, every fourth Sunday you may attend the
Curry Lunch. This is highly recommended because it
spares you the chore of cooking a roast. There are
always two sorts of curry on offer, mild chicken or hot
beef and you can usually tell which is which by their
colour. With it you will be offered a selection of 'bits'.
Don't make the mistake of thinking this is the fruit
salad for dessert.

In order to prepare you for the delights of the Army
functions you will have the pleasure of attending, I
will elaborate on some of them.

THE COCKTAIL PARTY

Of all the functions you will be required to attend,
there is probably nothing that you will enjoy less
than the annual cocktail party. Please note the
phrase, 'required to attend'. It's no good thinking that
you will be able to cry off with a headache; being in
hospital, attached to a life-support machine, having
been run over by a tank, is about the only acceptable
excuse. Still, if you can arrange it, you may find it
more pleasurable.

The idea of the annual Garrison/ Regimental/

Divisional cocktail party is to entertain and thank all those people who have supported and helped in the smooth running of the Garrison or Regiment or Division over the past year. In fact it doesn't seem to work like that and the people who end up coming are the ones with enough clout to wangle an invitation to get smashed at the Army's expense. (A euphemism for 'on your Mess Bill'.) The people you will see are not the ones who 'help' but the ones who could make life very uncomfortable all round if they wanted to. Thus you will have the pleasure of the company of the local MP, the editor of the local newspaper, the land owners, anyone whose house is anywhere near the ranges (just in case), the man from the Noise Abatement Society and so on. Almost without exception, none of these people will have the least thing in common with members of HM Forces and regard soldiers and their wives as if they have come from another planet. You can therefore imagine how scintillating the conversation is. Move the venue to an Army unit overseas, so there is the added attraction of a language barrier as well, and you may begin to see why attempted suicide is a soft option. The bosses know what they are up against when the order goes out to attend and their Staff are under strict instructions to regard any excuse for absence with total disbelief.

If you have children, your next problem (apart from finding a tank to throw yourself under) is to find a babysitter. None of your friends will be able to oblige, they are all going to the same do. The few nannies who are around will find themselves asked to look after their own charges plus fifteen other children, all tired and fractious because cocktail parties take place at the worst time of day for kids – between 6.00 and 8.00 p.m.

So imagine the scene, it is 5.00 p.m. and you have to feed and bathe the children before changing your own clothes and getting made up before 6.00 p.m. It's no good trying to be clever and sorting yourself out early. Unless you have an enormous plastic bag to swathe yourself in, you will look a complete wreck again by 6 o'clock. Besides which the children will know that something is afoot and immediately start to play you up, just to see you flip out completely. Having sorted yourself out, your husband arrives home with twenty minutes to get out of barrack dress, into a suit, shave, and fend off kids who are no longer clean. With minutes to spare you rush the kids to your friend's obliging nanny and sprint back home again to collect your husband, who has finished getting the poster paint off his trousers. Off you belt to the mess to affix a smile to your face and pour drink down the necks of complete strangers, who proceed to tell you how much they hate the Army.

The people who organise these events know precisely what would happen were everyone left to themselves; the party would split neatly into two halves, the Army down one end of the room and civilians up the other. In order to stop this happening, the guests are all allocated hosts who are under orders to look after their charges until they depart, or fall over. Who you get to host depends on how friendly your husband is with the Officer drawing up the list. If you get landed with the chicken farmer, whose hens have stopped laying because of the gunfire on the ranges, you can be certain that there is no love lost between them. However, get paired off with the squire who has a shoot and 300 yards of trout fishing, and you can begin to wonder whether your husband has caught the Adjutant/Staff Captain in some compromising position! Not that you are likely to get the squire to host; the Brigadier will bag that one for himself if he's got any sense.

The Army people are all briefed to arrive twenty minutes early. There are two reasons for this. The first is to make sure that the guests are certain of being hosted on their eventual arrival, and the second reason is to allow you to get a warmer into the bank. It helps thaw out the atmosphere somewhat and ensure that one or two of the smiles of welcome might almost be genuine. Otherwise the guests would quickly discover what it is like to walk into a deep freeze.

'A FROSTY RECEPTION'

The guests arrive and everyone struggles manfully to keep conversations going. Knowing absolutely nothing about chicken farming or noise abatement you find this an uphill task. However, the Mess waiters help you out by keeping the supply of gin and tonic flowing smoothly. There is also a procession of trays with canapés for you to offer your guest. These are particularly difficult to eat and it does mean that you can concentrate on that whilst madly trying to think up another conversational gambit. It's the same story for everyone, you can tell by the way they are talking to each other; the guests, who have not been briefed to stick like glue to one couple, are all looking over their hosts' shoulders, searching desperately for a friendly face, or possibly someone more important. At last your guest sees someone he knows and dashes off like a camel to an oasis, dragging his wife with him. This sets off a chain reaction, you are now free to wander and you move to help out your best friend who is struggling with the MEP. Your arrival allows the MEP to escape without feeling he is abandoning anyone and he can now search out the Friends of the Earth representative. Like dominos falling the reaction goes on around the room. Eventually the inevitable happens the party splits in two halves, us and them. By this time though, even the Brigadier has given up and is chatting to his pals about some exercise or other. The noise level in the room trebles and everyone begins to enjoy themselves.

By now it is 7.55 p.m. and the invitation firmly stated that cocktails were 6.00 – 8.00 p.m. Just as you start to relax and get into a really deep conversation about hair bows and boarding schools with your chums the drinks' supply switches off. As long as there is gin to drink the guests will stay, so the only way to get rid of them is to turn off the tap. Much more discreet than yelling 'time' it has exactly the same effect. Within minutes the Mess is clear apart from a snow drift of puff pastry flakes interspersed with the odd dollop of mushrooms in cream sauce. You are relieved to see that everyone found those damn canapés impossible to eat too.

Don't make the mistake of thinking that now is the moment to relax. You have been very abstemious all evening; just for a change you are driving home. Your task is to winkle your husband away from the bar (which has reopened now all the civvies have gone) and get him away from his boozy cronies. On no account should you give in and go home on your own. The kids, vile at 6.00 p.m., when you dumped them, will now be beyond everything. You must use this opportunity to show your husband just what they can be like. Besides which, the shock of seeing little Charlotte and Harry in their true colours will probably go some way towards sobering him up. And just think, you've only got a year to wait till the next cocktail party. Start looking for tanks now!

THE DINNER NIGHT

You will not be invited to this, but as you will have to cope with your husband both before and after the event, a few words of warning may prepare you for the worst.

This is a monthly occasion when your husband shoe-horns his way into his mess-kit and totters off to the Officers' Mess in order to eat himself to a standstill, play silly games and get plastered. (If the games are unduly boisterous then getting plastered may take place in the local hospital.) With the exception of the drink consumed, and that they sing rugby songs rather than 'Happy Birthday' it bears many resemblances to a four year old's bun fight.

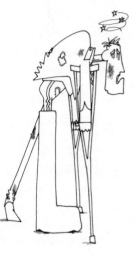

'...GETTING PLASTERED...'

You, on the other hand, are left at home with a scrambled egg and 'The Archers' for entertainment. But you have to work for this evening of unalloyed self indulgence. You start by helping your husband get into his mess-kit. For this you will need a large tin of axle grease and a straight face. Before attempting this task it is as well to reinforce the stitching of the seams and fly buttons with piano-wire, or its equivalent. It's best not to let your husband see you do this as it is bad for his morale. Since getting commissioned, a super-fit, sprightly nineteen year old has developed into a laid back captain with a paunch. Two stone can play havoc with the best tailoring. At this point the proceedings get

interesting; it's like watching strip tease in reverse.
Mess overalls (the proper name for the trousers) are
designed to be skin tight and having got them on, the
ankle boots (George Boots) can't be put on
afterwards. Thus trousers and boots have to be put on
simultaneously. A difficult feat now made harder by
paunch and tightness of trousers. You must not laugh
at his efforts, it causes a rise in blood pressure and
can jeopardise the entire operation, or possibly, even
his manhood. You will be required to do up laces, mop
brow and secure braces. (Not that there is much need
for these as trousers that took so much effort to get up
are unlikely to fall to the ground of their own
volition.) Now all you have to do is fix his cuff- links,
tie his bow tie and remove stains that he didn't spot
after the drunken bash. If you have been trained as a
Norland Nanny you will probably find this of help.
Finally as he is about to leave, one of the fly buttons
gives up the unequal struggle and pings off, giving
the cat a nasty fright and decapitates the azalea.
Too late for anything but a running repair with a
nappy pin, you can rest assured that he will be well
anaesthetised by the time that gives way.

You will now have seven peaceful hours before his
return. I can't over emphasise the importance of an
early night at this juncture. After 2.00 a.m. you will
be unlikely to get any more sleep. On his return,
invariably in the small hours, he should be able to
undress by himself as most of his clothes have been
loosened during the course of the evening by the loss
of buttons. Do keep an eye on him though, just to
ensure he does remove everything. I knew of a single
officer who, being so inebriated, gave up the struggle
with his boots and overalls. He awoke the following
morning in a room knee-deep in goose down. For a
while he thought that Bernard Matthews had

'STOP COMPLAINING, BY THE END OF THE EVENING IT WON'T
JUST BE YOUR TROUSERS THAT ARE TIGHT'

massacred an entire flock of turkeys in the Mess, but
eventually he was able to discover that his spurs had
ripped his expensive down duvet to shreds during his
sozzled sleep, and his drunken thrashings had
finished the job off.

'IT'S NOT JUST HIM THAT GETS HALF-CUT'

Having made sure that your husband has coped with the difficult bits, he will then repair to the kitchen for a fried egg sandwich. (It's as well to supervise again at this stage as it saves calling out the fire brigade later on.) You will then be regaled, incoherently, with the highlights of the meal and games while he gets into bed. (You may discover whose blood it is on his mess-kit as it patently isn't his, but if you don't one of the other wives will, and pass on the information. It's not that you really care but if the injury was very severe it may affect promotion prospects.) At this stage he will remember that, racked with guilt about all the lovely grub he's had to eat, he has bought you a present back from the Mess. Keep your excitement under control because it is most likely to be a packet of peanuts or a yorkie bar – just what you wanted at 2.00 a.m.

A split second before his head hits the pillow he will fall into a deep coma and begin snoring. These will be of the window rattling variety. Don't be foolhardy enough to believe you can stop them or sleep through them. Give in and go and sleep in the spare room.

This is part of Army life and you should not try to prevent it. I have known wives try to stop their husband from coming home completely blotto by nagging. It may work in the short term but they wise up to it. A favourite way round the problem is for the husband to rush in, yelling 'I'm home and I feel amazingly randy!' Which wives do you know who would brave doing anything else but feign deep sleep? The husband is then free to eat as many egg sandwiches as he wishes and no ear-bashing later.

THE LADIES GUEST NIGHT

Two or three times a year you will be allowed to accompany your husband to a formal dinner night in the Mess. If the Regiment is overseas this may be more often. If it is a really top class Regiment you may only get allowed in once in a blue moon and on special occasions – for example they may not wish the Queen to feel as though she is the odd one out. Depending on the whim of the Commanding Officer and the PMC (Master of Ceremonies) the dress may, or may not be, mess kit. Until you are conversant with the normal style of dress of the other wives you will find it difficult to judge exactly what to wear. Here are some tips.

Don't wear anything which is too revealing. A dress of this variety (a 'Bingo' dress; eyes down, look in) upsets senior Officers because it raises their blood pressure, and junior Officers because it raises their hopes. Similarly you should avoid a dress which will not adequately restrain you. Chernobyl dresses (lots of fall out) can cause upsets at the table particularly if you become over exposed during the soup course. And unless you are lucky enough to find that it is Vichyssoise on the menu it may be more than your face that goes red.

Do not wear anything too flamboyant and trendy unless you have a really extensive wardrobe. An outfit like this will cause a stir and will be remembered so you will be unable to ever wear it again whilst your husband is serving with the Regiment.

If you are not sure whether it is short or long dresses for the ladies, go for the ballerina style. Apart from the fact that it is very flattering, unless you have truly horrendous ankles and stand like a pigeon, and it will also allow you to ride home on your bike. This saves arguing with your husband about who's going to drive, an argument which you know you'll lose as he'll get drunk regardless.

Apart from dress there are some other conventions you will be expected to observe. You should be aware that Ladies are expected to retire from the table after the port has gone round. It is immaterial whether or not you have a desire to powder you nose or inspect the flower arrangement in the loo, leaving the room is compulsory. It is not a good idea to think that you can buck the system; if you do the Commanding Officer's wife will probably put you right, in no uncertain terms. Branded as some sort of trendy-pinko-lefty your husband's career may founder as a result of this seemingly innocent stand for women's rights. Remember, in the Army it's a man's world.

Whereas leaving the room after the meal is unavoidable, it is definitely frowned on during it. Should you not be blessed with the bladder of an elephant, you may have problems if you find that you are still at the table as the clock strikes midnight. Pregnant ladies are allowed to get away with trips to the lav, so you may be forced into telling a little white lie. (But for goodness sake warn your husband first if you think you may have to use this ploy. He may not relish having to buy a crate of bubbly for his mates so they can all celebrate the happy event, just because you couldn't 'hang-on'.) If you decide to brazen it out and pop to the loo regardless, beware of the subalterns. They find it a merry jape to spirit your chair away in your absence. And no amount of cajoling or threatening from you will get it back. One friend of mine was forced to kneel at table for dessert, speeches, port and coffee.

And whilst talking of port; never gulp it. Not that it looks unseemly, but you can be sure that if you do take a hefty belt there are going to be toasts to most of the heads of state in the universe. It does get noticed if you have to pretend to swig and there's nothing there.

Never get plastered. This is the prerogative of the men. Wives are really only invited to these do's in order to ensure that the men get home safely. Should you get tipsy do not make matters worse by joining in

the mens' songs or any of the Mess games. I once
knew a girl who challenged the CO to a drinking
match whilst standing on their heads. She forgot,
that once inverted, her dress would not defy gravity;
her husband has yet to recover from the
embarrassment of the entire Mess, and staff,
discovering what it was about her that he found so
attractive. She may not have remembered the
proceedings the next day, but everyone else did.

FITTING THE MOULD

Now that you have become a member of the patch you will have time to observe those around you. You will quickly notice how everyone has their own niche in the hierarchy. You will also learn that it is important to sport outward trappings of this position so that your position in the order of things is maintained. Nothing quite so flashy as an orb and sceptre is necessary; your clothes and pets should do the trick.

WHO'S WHO IN THE SYSTEM, AND HOW TO RECOGNISE THEM

1. The Garrison Commander: You will probably have no idea who this is as he will introduce himself to you as David. If he is amusing, (and they normally are) don't reciprocate with funny stories about your husband's faux pas in the Regiment. You will not have time to make an in depth assessment as your husband will drag you away before you drop a clanger.

His Wife: She won't know who you are – you're far too lowly. She will be recognisable by her immaculate hair and nails. Being a Brigadier's wife she gets 'house staff', which is enviable. She has to entertain endless boring people, which isn't. Her children have left boarding school and she spends most of her time being chairwoman of charitable committees. In her spare time, which is very limited, she plans tasks for other Officers' wives and jobs for her cleaner.

2. The Commanding Officer: He is always charming and remembers your name (although he doesn't know who your husband is). Out of uniform he wears a hound's tooth check sports jacket, cavalry twill trousers, striped shirt and Regimental tie. In his spare time he watches point-to-point races, which is as often as possible, and plays bridge. He also has a black labrador, a Volvo Estate and a flat cap.

His Wife: She can't remember your name. She has a delightful smile, used especially when asking you to run the jam stall at the Christmas Fund Raising Fair. She wears navy shoes, navy tights, Jaeger skirt, a lambswool sweater with a string of pearls and a head scarf carefully arranged around her neck. She also has a gold and diamond regimental brooch. She has three children at boarding school and does a lot of voluntary work – she is secretary of half a dozen charitable committees. Her spare time is spent doing tasks set by the Brigadier's wife.

3. The Officer Commanding: He will know both you and your husband and will talk to you until someone more important appears – almost anyone. He has a golden labrador, a Passat and his wife buys his shirts from Marks & Spencer. In his spare time he is learning to play bridge.

His wife: She wants promotion for her husband so she has lots of dinner parties and invites all the right people from the Staff List. This will not include you but you may be asked to a charity coffee morning if your luck's in. She wears a guernsey and her regimental brooch is only silver. She has two children at prep school and works as a supply teacher to help pay the fees. She is waiting to be invited onto a charitable committee. Her spare time is spent planning the menu for the next dinner party and clearing up from the last one.

'CLEARING UP FROM ONE DINNER PARTY AND ARRANGING THE NEXT'

4. A Captain: He has difficulty in remembering his own name. He earns very little but has signed for £9,000,000 of Army kit, including three tanks. His wife buys cords, check shirts and sweaters for him to wear. He has an MG, a spaniel, an overdraft and a wife. He doesn't get any spare time and if he does he is detailed to be Orderly Officer or to attend a cocktail party as part of rent-a-crowd.

His wife: You. You would like to wear jeans to the Mess but have been told you can't. You work full time, if only to avoid any charitable committees. You know your husband is in the Army, but you're not quite sure which bit, and not sure you ever want to. Your spare time is spent thinking up excuses not to go to coffee mornings or cocktail parties. You are also seeing if you can get your husband a better paid job – that means you have a lot of ground to cover.

5. The Sergeant Major: He doesn't have to know your name as he calls you Ma'am. He may be getting commissioned soon so he wears a flat hat and a dog tooth check jacket to get some practice in. He thinks that point-to-point is some sort of fancy needlework. He drives a Datsun and his children have a hamster. He has loads of spare time, no overheads and no problem with his blood pressure.

His wife: You meet her at the Wives' Christmas Do. She is very good at organising. She thinks Officers' wives are snobs, so there is nothing wrong with her powers of character assessment. She will never be on a charitable committee because she works full-time at Tescos. She earns more than your husband does, especially when she's on the late-night-shopping shift. You wish you could work there too but it clashes with your social life.

HUMOUR

An alternative way of working out where someone is in the social scale is by discovering how funny they are. (This is funny ha-ha not funny peculiar.) For this you must judge their humour by the reaction of those around them. It goes without saying that Brigadiers and above are 'very witty'. You will find that when listening to them, or their wives, their little anecdotes will be dutifully laughed at. You will be expected to perform this simple task, even if he has told you the story countless times before. If he starts the story off with 'I don't suppose I have told you about the time.......' on no account do you say 'Yes.'

If you are lower down the social scale than this you may tell jokes and stories, but you must be very careful about their content. Bawdy jokes are OUT. Real Officers' wives simply don't understand them; or if they do, they don't let on. Certainly, a junior Officer's wife should not dream of telling any sort of story, unless it is squeaky clean. Young wives are expected to be sweet, naïve and decorative, not robust, bawdy and rip-snortingly funny; those sort of girls are barmaids (and possibly a lot more fun).

While real Officers' wives are not expected to be humorous themselves they are expected to have a good sense of humour. This is often tested to the limit by their husbands. Good Officers' wives see the funny side when their husband returns home from being on exercise for four weeks. He arrives four hours late and throws stones at your bedroom window for you to let him in. You have long since put your silky nightie away and fallen asleep reading 'The Winds of War'. He finally succeeds in waking not only you but the entire family (he's not too worried about the neighbours – they're being woken up too). To placate a brood of screaming children he ends up sleeping in the spare room while you share your bed with restless children. In the morning you wake up to find his dirty kit strewn all over the house and a pack like the stone at Gethsemene blocking the door. When he eventually wakes up he tells you that when he's had a bath he'll be going gliding, sailing or rowing for the weekend. Being a good Officer's wife is not always easy.

PETS

Army Officers are, on the whole, addicted to the canine world. I think it stems from their downtrodden existence as subalterns; when they are being ordered around by everyone they seek solace in getting obedience from a dog. Besides which a huge number of Officers were brought up in the sort of houses which have vast numbers of gun dogs rampaging round and so, on joining their Regiment they take a dog along with them like a five year old takes a security blanket to school. But whatever the reason, dogs and Army Officers are inseparable. Breed of dog, when young and unattached, is not of paramount importance. Once married, and in the wider world of the patch, where the ground rules for being 'OK' are different, one must be careful to have just the right animal.

I have heard it said that when an Officer passes out of Staff College he gets issued with a black labrador. This is not the case. In fact the breed of dog says as much for its owner's Regiment as does his uniform. For example, those affiliated to Scottish Infantry Regiments will almost certainly be in possession of a Border Terrier, a Dandy Dinmont or possibly a Cairn. English Infanteers may well have a Labrador or Retriever, or possibly a Setter or Spaniel. Toy breeds are definitely unacceptable – 'large', 'working' or 'gun' should be applicable adjectives, otherwise it just isn't a suitable companion for a thrusting Officer.

When you get married you will no doubt find that, along with your husband, you will also be getting a dog. At this point it is essential for the novice wife to realise that, although it is *his* dog, you'll be the one who looks after it. He will spin you a yarn about how

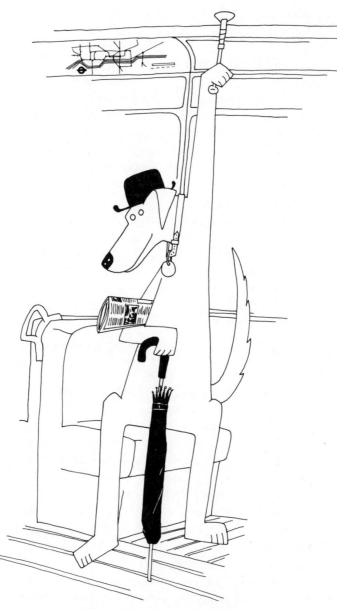

'IT'S A DOG'S LIFE AT MAIN BUILDING'

he'll take the dog to work ..... Don't fall for it. When
was the last time you saw a labrador strap-hanging
on the 0750 train to Waterloo? And if he isn't
commuting to MOD it's unlikely that he'll be able to
train the beast to ride pillion on his racing bike.
Whatever it is that he tries to con you into believing,
you can rest assured that it will be you taking
Killer/Buster/Fido for a three mile hike twice a day.

If you were not brought up in a doggy house you
may be at a loss to see what benefit these creatures
are to human-kind. Man's best friend – fine – you can
grasp that; but on a wet winter's morning when you
dash back from walking the kids to school, in order to
trek round Hampstead Heath, and then rush back
home to sort out the dog's and the childrens'
lunches..... definitely not woman's best friend. But
many wives have been converted. When your
husband goes away for six months, opening a tin of
Pal can be a small price to pay for a friend to fill up the
empty space in your bed. In fact, after a few months
you may prefer the dog.

The other alternative to possessing a dog is to own
a horse. Certainly this is a must for those Officers in
Cavalry Regiments. During the day, your husband
will be busy at work, so you can be certain that it will
be you doing the mucking-out, feeding and
exercising. And don't think that having two small
children and a double buggy to cope with will let you
off the hook. Your husband will help out at weekends
so that you can catch up with the week's housework.
If postings or penury makes horse ownership
impossible, and you want to ensure social
acceptability, then enrolling little James or Camilla
in the Pony Club, and being a regular helper with
Riding for the Disabled, will probably just about do.
You should be able to fit this in, in the spare hour left

between walking the dogs and getting the kids from school. That is, if you don't need to wash the kitchen floor around the dogs' bowls each day, and shovelling out the back garden takes less than ten minutes.

For those people who are unfortunate enough to be attached to one of the Corps, it is probably better not to bother with a dog. It can lead to accusations of social climbing. A cat or a gerbil is much more suited to your status and in some cases a goldfish is the only possible option.

Of course, once your husband reaches the dizzy heights of being a senior Officer, it really doesn't matter what you have as a pet. By the time he has gained his red tabs others will look upon your pet duck, or rattle snake, as a manifestation of mild, but harmless eccentricity and no one will think any the less of you. Try it as a lowly Captain and his wife and ostracism will be swift. Having a really unusual pet (an iguana or a baboon) might cause you some

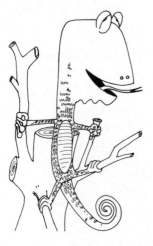 

'FROM ONE CHAMELEON TO ANOTHER, I REALLY DON'T THINK KHAKI'S YOUR COLOUR'

problems, especially as they do say that owners grow to look like the animals they keep.

One of the many headaches caused by owning a pet is that it can cost a fortune to quarantine them following an overseas tour. This is a rule that does not apply to the equine world – the Cavalry probably used their influence on this one – but all other small warm-blooded creatures must spend six months in solitary and very expensive confinement for the pivilege of rejoining their owners in UK. (For some reason, children are exempt from this too.) Therefore, there are numerous Officers who refuse the delights of an overseas tour for the sake of their pets. Those Officers in the right sort of Regiments receive a sympathetic ear and the furthest east they can expect to serve is Colchester. Should this fail, then for the duration of the two year tour the childrens' child benefit is carefully saved in order to pay for Rover's quarantine.

USING THE NAAFI

Before I knew any better I once asked someone 'What is this thing called the NAAFI?' She replied 'Oh, it means Never 'As Any Fink In.' I was no wiser.

I have since discovered that the NAAFI represents an organisation which runs a chain of corner shops and supermarkets hidden away in garrisons and other Army strongholds. The stocking of these shops is designed to meet the needs of the Army population they serve. Quite sensible. Consequently they have shelves of every kind of beer in the world, disposable razors, Durex, TV dinners and tins of meat. Market research on the female part of their market is more limited. As a result everything they sell is 'one size only' from tights to tampons. It's not quite true to say that they're empty, they just never seem to have anything that you want.

I suppose NAAFI, sometimes spelt Naffy is the origin of a growth area in the English language. 'Naf' meaning a load of rubbish is a fair description of many of the consumer items found in such stores. 'Naf off' is the sort of reply you could expect from complaining about them. 'Naafia' refers to the monopolies their shops have both at home and overseas and the kind of strongarm tactics they use for ensuring their credit bills are paid. There's no need to worry about your darling husband Nigel refusing to pay your bills. He'll be hauled up in front of his senior Officer if he defaults so much as a deutchmark. If he still refuses to pay after what he calls a 'bollocking', then there's always a court martial and the firing squad. If it goes that far he will be just the teensie weensiest bit cross with you.

You will hear many Officers' wives complaining about their NAAFI. However, it is worth considering the advantages of using your NAAFI both at home and abroad.

THE NAAFI AT HOME

Shopping at the NAAFI is really part of your job as your husband's wife. Buying trolley loads at Waitrose or Sainsburys may be necessary to feed your family, but a good Officer's wife will need to make regular trips to the NAAFI as well. Shopping in the NAAFI is rather like being a policeman on the beat. You can chat to your husband's soldiers' wives and let them know who you are. Most of them will probably have guessed already which is something to do with the way you are dressed. Even if you don't learn the truth about what is really going on (soldiers' wives smiles and pleasant remarks hide a thousand juicy bits of scandal and naughty goings on) you will at least be able to find out what soldiers eat for their supper. This is very valuable 'intelligence' and it may throw some light on why you had so much chilli con carne left over when you last gave a lunch for the other ranks.

If you live on an Army camp the NAAFI is usually very close by. Your children can pester you all day for a walk to the NAAFI so that you can buy them sweets. Having a local NAAFI does at least have a few advantages. You can wander around looking for things to buy. It's usually a very cheap shopping trip and it is warmer than window shopping. If you desperately need a birthday present for a children's party, you can always be sure that the NAAFI will have a good stock of Christmas gifts right through the year, although the chocolates are a bit of a giveaway when they are covered in white powder.

Shopping in the NAAFI does have its price to pay. Unless your children are very well trained you will have to endure the ritual argument over sweets. Naturally they are strategically placed at the exit to force people to buy them against their will. When you refuse, your children will writhe all over the floor screaming, and show you up in front of the other ranks. You'll seriously wonder why you bothered to come out in the first place. At least you could have finished off your flower arrangement for the Mess.

Most NAAFIs have a pretty favourable staff to customer ratio. The customers they have are usually only there to buy a packet of cigarettes and to discuss their latest hysterectomy in public. On the whole you shouldn't have to wait at the checkout for too long for the staff to finish their tea break or dusting the shelves. The point about shopping in the NAAFI is that there is no rush. The staff don't rush about being busy otherwise the Manager would make cuts and sack their friends. They like to save their customers up. Just like they save up the jobs of stocking the shelves and tidying the trolleys. That way they can always find something to do to look as though they are busy when the manager returns from his lunch in the Mess.

In recent years the NAAFI has changed its policy towards its customers. They seem to have realised that they need them. They could have cut their prices and increased their range of goods to halt the flood of wives traipsing to distant supermarkets. (The sight of buses to Army camps, steamed up and full of bags of shopping, screaming children and babies is still not a thing of the past.) Instead they are keeping some of their shops open late in the evening. This is actually very useful if you run out of tonic water when it's time for drinkies. You can send your husband out and do a very non-Officer's wife thing. Put your feet up and watch the TV.

THE NAAFI ABROAD

Some NAAFIs abroad are like supermarkets and others like department stores (well almost). It's abroad that they excel in having the monopoly of a truly English speaking establishment supplying British goods. Where else could you buy pork and beef chipolata sausages, Marks and Spencer underwear and paintings of the Cotswolds in Cyprus, Hong Kong or Germany?

By using the NAAFI you can avoid any contact with the local population. You need never buy their food nor speak their language. This probably comes as a bit of a relief if you are not a born linguist. Although the Army does run courses for you to become a German speaker or whatever you will be unlikely to find the time. Let's face it, there are more enjoyable things to do abroad than learn the language. Unfortunately you will have to make some concessions to living abroad. You still can't buy NAAFI goods in pounds sterling.

Based on your experience of shopping in the NAAFI at home, service is reliably predictable. On a shopping day you need never plan to do anything else. It will take you all day to get to the NAAFI, park, shop, queue and drive home. It's worth remembering that the NAAFI abroad is really the meeting place of all the ranks. More than anything it is important to dress well for the NAAFI and talk to your husband's soldiers' wives. Timing is most important. It's worth doing this quite conspicuously as you can be sure his senior Officers' wives will make a note of your efforts. After all they are there for precisely the same reason and will find time to chat to you.

On some overseas postings you must show your identity card before you are allowed to enter the NAAFI. This is a great thrill and means you can leave any boring visitors from UK outside. While they are hanging around outside you can buy all the food past its sell by date to give them for supper. If a bout of food poisoning doesn't send them back early, at least they'll stop eating and drinking your cupboard bare. They're probably under the misapprehension that duty free means given away free.

'...AND IF YOU'RE GOOD I'LL BRING YOU A PACKET OF CHOC DROPS'

'RELAXING IN THE NAAFI CAFI'

At the end of your shopping trip, when you have loaded your car and before you tackle driving on the wrong side of the road, you may be tempted to the café for a quiet sit down and a cup of tea. If your NAAFI does have a cafeteria be warned; this is nothing like the cafeteria in John Lewis'. You will be in danger of sticking to the sweet tea covered floor. That is, if you can see your way in through the fog of smoke. No smoking campaigns are a waste of time in the Army abroad when cigarettes are bought in boxes of 200. People need walk-in larders just for their cigarettes and booze – duty free of course. There are limits to your duty free allowances. These allowances are based on what an alcoholic smoker would get through in a month. Only the hospital cases or doctors ever reach their allowance.

WORKING WIVES

If you want to be a real Officer's wife, don't even think of working. Well-trained wives, those born to it like Cavalry and Guards wives, wouldn't dream of it. In fact, to maintain the truly correct image you ought to employ a nanny and a cleaner too. Senior wives get house staff provided for them at government expense, and if you want your husband to get you to these dizzy heights, you must sacrifice your career right from the start. When he is well on his way up the ladder you can probably go back to work without causing too much damage to his prospects. This being the case, as you have got to stay at home in the early years, you might just as well have children. Then, when his position is pretty unassailable, you can pack your offspring off to boarding school and pick up the threads again. But if you feel you must work, you will find this is a wonderful way of avoiding all those charity sales and committee meetings. Besides which it helps out with the cash flow problem.

JOB HUNTING AT HOME

Here are some tips for job hunting in the UK:

1. Never mention that your husband is in the Army. A prospective employer will know that you are bound to be posted as soon as you have settled in. Try saying

that you are separated; if he's on exercise a lot you won't really be lying.

2. If you are job hunting around Aldershot or Catterick or any big garrison, don't use a euphemism like 'Government Servant' to describe your husband's employment; they wised up to that one years ago. Try, demolition expert; after all, that's what he does if we go to war, isn't it?

3. Remember that only professional jobs are socially acceptable to your new found status; for instance nursing, teaching, cordon-bleu catering or interior design. The oldest profession does NOT count.

4. If you are required to produce a CV you may have to lie about your age. To make it look as though you don't move house quite so frequently and that you have stayed several years in each previous job, you may have to add on a decade.

5. It is perfectly acceptable to run a business from home providing that you are selling designer knitwear, childrens books, party cakes or hand painted nursery pictures. Don't expect other Officers' wives to patronise your venture; they're far too busy flogging their own stuff. Never run a catalogue, sell naughty undies or do hairdressing. Remember that as a member of the ruling class you should leave that to the proletariat.

JOB HUNTING OVERSEAS

This is altogether a different kettle of fish. In the UK your civilian employer doesn't give a damn about rank and social status. In fact, you will have hidden from him that you are anything to do with the Army at all. In Germany, or anywhere else overseas for that matter, your only possible employer (unless you are a linguist) is the Army. Rank is now of utmost importance and you will find that only certain jobs are considered acceptable to your status. You may long to be a check out girl on a NAAFI till but there are those who will protect you from yourself. You will be firmly told that Officers' wives may not apply and you will be steered towards something more appropriate, like lab assistant, irrespective of the fact that you can't even spell laborito... laboratr...lab, much less assist in one.

So here are some tips for getting a job outside Britain:

1. Sign on at the British Labour Exchange immediately if you can find it. They are well hidden. They used to be called the PCLU but are now PLSU, neither name is designed to enlighten you. It all adds to the mystique.

2. Have a CV ready to hand in. You can then copy all the details on to one of their forms. Make sure you keep a copy for when they lose the lot.

3. Don't be surprised to be sent for interviews for jobs for which you are totally unqualified. Most of the others who turn up are in the same boat so you may get the job after all.

4. Remember that you will only find the perfect job, and be offered it, when you are due to return to UK within the month.

POSTINGS

PREPARING TO MOVE

The system that you have married into has a wonderful knack of mind reading. The minute you express contentment with your lot, even if it is only to yourself, a posting order will come winging onto your husband's desk. Find yourself happy with your house, get the children settled into nursery and school, make friends and get a job, and you can be sure of a posting to Germany or the Hebrides before the month is out. The Army kids you along that most postings are for three years. You might get two years in one spot if you're lucky, or if your husband really hates his job. Your civilian friends quickly realise how often you move. They give up having to snopaque their address book; after knowing you for more than four years they resort to giving you a loose-leaf.

Your husband may be warned that he is due for a posting and be given a form to fill out so that he can express his preference for his next job. This is known as the 'dream sheet'. And we all know that dreams never come true. Some people believe that the Army always gives you the complete opposite to what you have asked for. They therefore ask for Aldershot in the hope that they will get Hong Kong. Naturally enough they get exactly what they have asked for –

Aldershot. Try the direct approach and ask for Hong Kong and where do you get sent? Yes, Aldershot. I have friends who reckon postings are decided by the throw of a dart at a board. That is probably about the most accurate guess at the workings of the system although the Brass assure everyone that logic, planning and a great deal of thought goes into each and every posting. I still think they use a dart board.

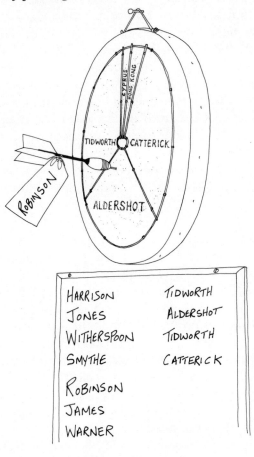

'THE POSTINGS GAME'

THE MARCH OUT

When you got married and moved into your new
quarter you were blissfully unaware of all the
bureaucracy of the move. Your husband handled that
before the wedding. You might have thought that all
it involved was handing over the keys; just a down
market version of the 'Ceremony of the Keys'. Not so.
You'll quickly learn from other wives exactly what
you are in for. For first-timers, the thought of a move
is daunting. Your neighbours will all helpfully tell
you that along with a bereavement and divorce, it is
the most stressful thing you can do. Being up to the
eyes in Valium or gin doesn't improve things but at
least you won't care. If it was just moving all your
goods and chattels it wouldn't be so bad, but the fun
starts when you clean the house for 'march out'. A
march out is when your house gets inspected for
damage and cleanliness, prior to being handed over
to a new tenant. And it is every bit as dreadful as it
sounds.

These days things are getting pretty enlightened;
no longer do the men from the PSA go round with
white gloves on. The laundry bills must have risen
too high, they just use their hands instead to check for
dust in every conceivable nook and cranny. Stand
still too long and you could find that you are marked
down as a reject. The inspection of the oven is the
most ghastly part. What other institution would
expect wives to make a twenty year old cooker look as
though it had just left the showroom? By the time you
have finished cleaning it, all you really want to do is
lie down with your head in it. Because of the horrors
of the inspection people have resorted to desperate
measures to avoid having faults in the house spotted

on their departure. Cracked washbasins have been known to have toothpaste or snopaque artistically applied, mattresses dusted with talcum powder to hide a stain, one friend of mine even got her husband to sand blast parts of her oven to make them pass inspection. (The fact that the oven was probably permanently damaged after that was of less importance than the fact that it was clean.)

'IF YOUR LUCK'S REALLY OUT IT'LL BE ELECTRIC'

So having waved goodbye to the removal van, and said farewell to your spotless house you now have the delightful prospect of the journey to your new home. If this is across the Channel and you are accompanied by small children you will understand why most people in the Army have an estate car. Being homeless for a couple of days, and knowing that you are going to have to survive in your new home for up to a week before your kit arrives, the only thing you won't have crammed into the car is the kitchen sink. Toys, nappies, bedtime stories, favourite teddies, a kettle, the left overs from your store cupboard, two or three suitcases. It's a lot to squeeze into a Golf Gti. You'll promise yourself a Passat or a Volvo Estate as soon as you arrive.

'I TOLD YOU, IF WE'D PACKED THE CHILDREN IN THE VAN
WE COULD HAVE FITTED MORE DUTY-FREE IN'

MARCHING IN

Having arrived at your new quarter you must now go through the 'march in' before you can unload your car and sort out your screaming children from the debris of the journey. In fact this isn't half as traumatic as a 'march out' but when you come to take over your first quarter you are not to know this. In layman's terms the march in is when you see your new home for the first time. You are introduced to it by the man from the PSA in the presence of the out-going occupant. You then play the excruciatingly embarrassing game of saying why you think the quarter is dirty, demanding to know what the marks on the mattresses are and asking what the smell is. The Officer vacating it has to explain the faults away. If you win, he foots the bill to have everything brought up to standard. If you don't, you have to do the explanations for the next tenants when it's your turn to move out.

The problem is that when you are moving into a quarter it is probably at the end of a long journey, you are tired and you are not up to the sort of detective work required to spot all the devious little measures to cover up the faults. Consequently they only come to light some months later, and rather than footing the bill, you too resort to snopaque, talcum powder and the like. And while you're at it you might just as well move the wardrobe a bit to cover up that unfortunate mark where you spilt your coffee. And so it goes on. That is, until some poor unfortunate person gets caught because the whole house, held together by bodge-tape and super glue, disintegrates before their very eyes.

Of course one thing which must be said is that no Officers' wife ever moves into a quarter which she considers 'Really Clean' but she always leaves her last one 'Absolutely Spotless'. So who makes them dirty between occupants?

LIVING OVERSEAS

'Join the Army and see the world' say the recruiting posters. What they don't say is that 'the world' is a euphemism for north-west Germany. In the course of your married life you will see a lot of Germany. Well, a lot of some bits of it at any rate. The Army make it sound more exotic by calling it BAOR, but there isn't any way that anyone can make the Luneberger Heath glamourous. The British Army was given that bit of Germany to play with after the war; the Yanks got the Black Forest and Heidleberg, the Belgiques the pretty bit around the Möhne See, and what did we get? The Rhur. Home from home if you come from Merseyside. But look on the bright side, it's handy for the cross-Channel Ferries.

You will very quickly discover that the exotic postings always go to other people. It is still possible to serve in Cyprus, Gibralter, Hong Kong, Nepal and so on. But you can bet your life that if you long to travel, if your husband volunteers for these postings at every opportunity, if you pack your kids off to boarding school so that there is no excuse not to go, then your postings will alternate between Aldershot, Catterick and Fallingbostel (known to all who have been stationed there as F...ing B..... , which sums it up nicely).

Despite the attraction of warmer climes, serving in Germany does have some definite advantages. For a start, it is an ideal way of getting away from your relatives. Once safely ensconced over the Channel it is too far for them to 'pop over for the weekend'. On your first posting there they may get enthusiastic and rush over like little lemmings to visit you for a holiday. If you are careful not to make their stay too

exciting, you can be fairly certain that you can curtail
their enthusiasm for subsequent trips. Send them on
German railways a couple of times with 2nd class
tickets and you shouldn't see too much of them in
future.

Petrol, drink and cigarettes are all duty-free in
Germany for the troops and their families. I find it
hard to come to terms with this when you consider
that the Army likes to project itself as a fit, healthy,
fighting machine that can yomp for miles across
hostile territory. Where is the incentive to give up the
little indulgences that make them soft? Still, if you do
smoke and drink, it is nice to get it on the cheap. You
also get some extra cash for living overseas. It used to
be quite a tidy sum which made life very pleasant
indeed. The MOD have now wised up to this, the
inevitable cuts have been made, and they can't
understand why people don't want to go there any
longer. Perhaps they feel that escaping from one's
relatives for a few years is reward enough.

The highlight of living overseas is, of course,
getting to know the locals. You may find that the
language barrier restricts your progress in
international relations to begin with. Try speaking
very slowly and loudly to them, they usually
understand quite quickly that you want them to
learn English. After all, we did win the war, didn't
we?

Some people go to great lengths to learn German.
The Army even puts on courses. This is a good way of
getting to meet some of the single soldiers if you are a
bored housewife. But you may not find the German
taught to be quite what you need. Phrases like 'I want
to requisition this barn' or 'I accept your offer of
unconditional surrender' aren't much use in the local
supermarket when you want to find out the cost of

tomatoes. Personally I would advise against these courses. Once it becomes known that you can speak the lingo you will get stuck with going to all sorts of dreary functions where you are expected to help entertain foreign nationals. Much better to avoid these do's as it takes you away from the cut and thrust of the British social life where you can help advance your husband's career.

If you enjoy skiing Germany is a good place to be. You may find that your husband is even ordered to go skiing for two weeks in the Bavarian Alps. At this point it is vital that you import a relative to look after the kids while you nip off there too. If they are old enough to go with you so much the better but still take Granny along so you can enjoy the après-ski.

If you enjoy driving then Germany is not for you. Inside each patriotic German is a fighter pilot waiting to escape. Once in their huge great Mercs, their alter ego takes over. They may not have won the Battle of Britain but they're not going to let the Battle of the Autobahn go the same way. In your British car you are legitimate quarry, as far as they are concerned, however inoffensive and law-abiding you are. It is their Teutonic duty to carve you up and reduce you to a gibbering wreck in the shortest possible distance.

Germans are also sticklers for the law. If the speed limit says 50km/h then that is the speed they will drive at; undaunted by rain, fog, ice, snow or even traffic jams, they will travel at the correct speed. The British authorities in Germany try to help you by making you learn the German highway code before you are allowed on their roads. It is a kind thought, but there is no substitute for being thrown in at the deep end – especially when the waters are shark infested.

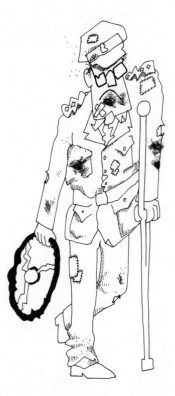

'THE BATTLE OF THE AUTOBAHN'

There are other places to get posted. Cyprus is especially lovely. Unfortunately, it is a bit of an elephants' graveyard – if you do get sent there you know that your husband's chances of further promotion are as good as a snowball's chances in Hell. So if you are really keen on climbing the ladder you must bite the bullet and eschew the nice places.

THE SOCIAL LIFE

HOW TO SURVIVE A COFFEE MORNING

Coffee mornings are the hub of an Officer's wife's social life. At around 10.30 a.m. Officers' wives generally get together for a cup of coffee and a chat. It's an opportunity to meet other wives of your rank before you meet them formally at dinner parties. For most Officers' wives the coffee morning will be the first function of the day, and in a busy schedule of luncheon, shopping, tea and cocktails it's a good chance to wake yourself up to the important job of socialising.

There aren't coffee mornings every day. Every other day is enough. Otherwise there wouldn't be time for shopping and organising charity stalls. Beware of things called 'Lace Parties' and 'Skin Care Parties'. These may sound like coffee mornings when you're invited and may even feel like them when you're tucking into the chocolate cake and coffee. However there's always a price to be paid and it could be three tablecloths or a face pack.

When you're very tied up it's worth distinguishing the kind of coffee mornings you've been invited to. There are 'Formal Coffee Mornings'. These are usually held in a senior Officer's wife's house or if they can't face it, it'll be in the Mess. Attendance is virtually compulsory and you can rely on other

Officers' wives to land you right in it if you skive off. It's a bit like taking Mass or Communion. If you can't make it to a coffee morning you can be sure people will be calling on you to check on your well being.

You might find coffee mornings a bit of a bore, after all they involve standing for hours in a hot stuffy room balancing a cup of cold coffee with a biscuit and a handbag. But they do involve mixing with senior Officers' wives. This is vital for your husband's career. The most dangerous kind of senior Officers' wives usually prowl round these sorts of affair. They ask you what you are interested in and before you know it they've got their diary out and you're booked to give a demonstration to their flower club or run a stall at the Guild of Saint Helena charity do. It takes a special kind of wife to keep a smile on her face, when she's done her stint at a coffee morning, been lemonned to do the flowers in the children's ward at the local hospital and then her husband accuses her of sitting around drinking coffee all day.

'Informal Coffee Mornings' are a much friendlier affair. They are an opportunity to mix with Officers' wives of your own rank. There's usually lots of gossip about senior Officers and their wives or anybody else who isn't there. Only foolish wives dare to confide the details of their private lives or sexual gymnastics with the hostess of a coffee morning, or any other Officer's wife for that matter. Come to think of it, it would be more discreet to walk around the streets of Camberley or London wearing a placard with the words 'ONLY THE SAS CAN BONK ALL NIGHT' than mention anything to another Officer's wife. Coffee mornings are an essential part of the 'Army Grapevine' (which is similar to the bush telegraph or any other means of communication that doesn't involve British Telecom).

...THE CHANDELIER BROKE AND WE FELL NAKED ONTO

"Only the SAS can BONK all night!"

'....JUST A WHISPER IN YOUR EAR....'

It's worth arriving armed with a bit of scandal. If you haven't any and haven't the imagination to make up any, the name and birth weight of the latest arrival to the Garrison or patch population will get you noticed, at least for a second or two. The other main topic of conversation is which dinner party you went to last night. If you're not on the main dinner party circuit it's a good idea to go out on your own to rather obscure restaurants and pubs. That way you give the illusion of having a full engagement calendar. (Some wives put down regular things like their aerobics class or visits to the hypnotherapist. This is a bit low and should be avoided.) It's not entirely compulsory to go to an informal coffee morning, but if you skip too many you will get a reputation for being anti-social and won't get in on the dinner party circuit. All in all this won't do your husband's career any good.

'Coffee Parties' are an altogether different sort of engagement. They are usually held by Officers' wives who haven't got anything better to do with their time.

These coffee parties make you feel obliged to buy something you either don't want or wouldn't ever dream of wanting. It is rather ludicrous to buy a face mask to cleanse your skin when you have a mouth full of chocolate cake. These are coffee mornings to avoid unless you have nothing better to do.

DRESS FOR COFFEE MORNINGS

It's a good idea to dress for coffee mornings, or for anywhere else for that matter. But when invited to a 'Formal Coffee Morning', dress is paramount. You will probably have been asking the question 'What shall I wear?' since childhood. At least with the Army, once you've learnt the rules you can relax. What is 'de rigueur' for an Officer's wife is almost timeless. Frilled shirts and Gucci shoes will be 'in' long after yours have worn out. Your problem will be replacing them when they've been out of fashion for a decade or two.

At 'Formal Coffee Mornings' you will probably be mixing with some pretty senior wives. It's best not to draw too much attention to yourself and the day wear uniform should be worn. Pearls are a must with your Laura Ashley frilled blouse, navy sweater, dark tailored skirt, navy tights and Gucci shoes. That way you will feel less intimidated should the Brigadier's wife speak to you. Make sure your shoes are really comfortable. It's unlikely that you will be given the chance to sit down. This enables the senior wives to circulate freely and prevents them getting stuck with anyone who's boring.

CHILDREN AND COFFEE MORNINGS

If you are unfortunate enough to have young children not yet in pre-prep on no account take them to a 'Formal Coffee Morning'. More experienced Officers' wives will have nannies or au pairs for just this kind of occasion. If your husband is not in the Guards and can't run to a nanny you'll have to park them with someone for the morning. Don't count the cost of the favour. Anything is better than having your little blighters stuff jammy dodgers into the Brigadier's wife's handbag and then wipe their fingers on the hem of her skirt.

'Informal Coffee Mornings' are not quite as strict as their formal counterparts. You will probably be allowed to sit down and you may bring your children. If, after living on a patch or Garrison for a while, you find them a trifle tedious then the best thing to do is to hold your own. Invite a lot of wives at once to be as sociable as possible and then hide in the kitchen all morning, brewing coffee and listening to Radio 4. When you're scraping up the chocolate cake that's been ground into the carpet remember that coffee mornings are an ideal way of entertaining people you don't know or whose husbands you don't like. You'll be invited out to a lot more supper parties as a result.

THE DINNER PARTY

In order to really ensure that your husband has a top quality chance in the promotion stakes it is important to have dinner parties for all the people who may be able to help in this. It is your duty to hold dinner parties. Remember, in the Army it's not 'What you know' but 'Who you know' that counts. The duty dinner party has all the inevitability of sex after a Victorian Maiden's wedding, and about as much enjoyment. But there is no point in kicking and screaming, you might just as well think of England and get on with it because there is no escape.

Whilst most of the human race is fairly gregarious and sociable, Officers' wives have made a science out of entertaining. Supper, with a couple of good friends, around the kitchen table over a meal of hot pot and a bottle of plonk, is out. For a start, a couple of friends are unlikely to be in a position to advance your husband's career. Furthermore, if you have five couples to dinner, that means you are owed five return matches; and that means five possible opportunities of meeting People-Who-Matter who might be of assistance to your husband's career. Now in order not to sound too ambitious (that would never do) a well-trained Officer's wife shrugs off these mega-dinner parties with 'Oh! It's not really any bother, it's no more effort to cook for twelve than two you know.' You and I know that anyone who says that is either out of their tree or they've had the caterers in.

Frankly, cooking for twelve people is a nightmare, especially in an Army kitchen, some of which look as though they were modernised to celebrate the defeat of Napoleon. So, unless your name is Shirley Conran or you really are a cordon bleu cook (and to be fair, there are some of those around) a dinner for twelve is Hell. To make matters even worse you can be pretty certain that the success or failure of your efforts is going to discussed the next day around the patch. If you serve up something that is absolutely disgusting you know that the other wives are all having a good laugh about it before you have finished the washing up the following morning. (The reason that you personally are doing the washing up, and not a machine, is because in the ante-diluvian kitchen there is nowhere to put one!)

One fairly good way of steering through the hazards of a dinner party is to get everyone sloshed early on in the evening so that they either don't care what they are eating or they won't be able to remember. You also have the added bonus that your guests will have such a massive hangover that they won't wish to see anyone else on the patch for several days, by which time, with any luck, there's been another dinner party so your own debacle is old news.

However, the real Officer's wife doesn't resort to these tactics. For a start the top drawer wives don't really approve of heavy drinking, and if their husbands aren't allowed to get smashed then why should anyone else? To be a success as an Officer's wife you must have supreme confidence in your own abilities as a cook. You must be able to survive a real culinary disaster. When the dinner you've prepared should really be consigned to the dog (and subsequently the bin when the dog spurns it too), you must be able to carry on regardless. Just go round the table offering your guests 'some of this delicious goo!' Of course they are all too stunned, or polite, or busy talking to refuse. If you do it with sufficient aplomb everyone ends up believing that the food really was good and the other wives clamour for the recipe.

Officers' wives have a strict code of what is acceptable at a dinner party. It almost goes without saying that Mateus Rose and Le Piat d'Or are not on the list of wines on offer. Neither are avocados (except in green salads) either with or without prawns in pink sauce, lots of different gateaux covered in

'A PLOMB PUDDING'

cream, or anything with offal. Like all things, dinner parties are subject to fashions. One influential wife saying 'I went to so-and-so's the other evening and the meal was wonderful; so simple and elegant. She was SO clever, we had Iles Flottantes for pudding,' condems everyone to meringue in custard for the next six weeks. Then, thank goodness someone comes up with a new delight.

There are some things that do make it easier to have big dinner parties. For a start, unless you have your own furniture, the Army thoughtfully issues you with a table that will seat eight comfortably, and ten at a squeeze. Some people, mainly the more ambitious Officers' wives, also have a matching card table (essential for bridge parties). It can also be used to extend the table to such a degree that you can stick all the people you don't like down one end so you are left to concentrate on the People-Who-Matter at your end. Those poor souls who haven't been promoted to the dizzy heights of Major are deemed only to have a few friends and no need to entertain lavishly so they only get issued with six dining room chairs. Once you get past this stage you are allowed a few more.

'IF YOU NEED BINOCULARS TO SEE YOUR HOSTESS THEN YOU REALLY ARE AT THE BOTTOM OF THE SOCIAL SCALE'

Naturally all these guests need knives and forks to

say nothing of vast quantities of glasses and crockery. Gone are the days when the Army issued it all to you. Not that most Officers' wives needed it anyway. If you have the right sort of wedding you will end up with lots of lovely Royal Worcester, Stuart crystal and canteens full of silver. You might also get some candelabra, nothing too ostentatious, plus some little silver flower vases because you 'couldn't possibly have people round without flowers!'

The Officer's wife prides herself on being the Perfect Hostess. The downstairs loo will be clean, with towels free from grubby little hand prints, there will be a new bar of soap and possibly even some flowers. Her guests needn't suffer the embarrassment of yelling through the locked door for more loo roll, a spare will certainly be there. She will ensure that there is enough space in the hall cupboard for all her guests' coats and sufficient hangers to hang them on. She will not, like ordinary mortals, wait until her visitors have moved into the sitting room and then chuck the coats, in a heap, over the banister rail. Her children do NOT appear in the middle of the proceedings to announce the need to 'do a Poo Mummy!' Nor does she have a complete sense of humour failure when her husband fails in his duties with the G&Ts because he is too busy talking shop with his boss. Moreover, when she serves the food it still looks edible even if dinner was delayed two hours due to the late arrival of guests who couldn't get their children to bed. You can also be certain that she is not going to happily dole out ten helpings only to discover that both she and another guest are left with empty plates. Finally when she eats, her food is either on her plate, her fork or in her mouth. It does not end up down her front – it wouldn't dare! If you can do all this then you are a true Officer's wife.

Once the meal is over no dinner party is complete
without a few games. Until recently Trivial Pursuits
was very popular, especially with senior Officers.
Many of them have good memories so by mugging up
the answers the night before they could guarantee a
victory and therefore prove their natural superiority.
Then some junior Officers started doing the same
thing and spoilt all the fun. It does seem though that
the higher ranking the Officers the more daring the
games after dinner. No Captain would dream of
introducing a game of Feathers. Colonels and above
however think it is great sport. I was introduced to
the game of Feathers by a Brigadier; in this game
everyone sits in a circle on the floor holding the edge
of a sheet against their chin, a feather is placed in the
middle and the idea is to blow it off the sheet.
Whoever is nearest when it goes over the edge must
remove a piece of clothing. So there we all were,
semi-clad when the door-bell rang. All the junior
Officers had visions of the News of the World
headlines and there was an undignified dash to
retrieve lost trousers from under the sheet. As it was
there was no news hound panting at the door on the
scent of front-page scandal, merely a passing
Samaritan wishing to find the owner of a car with its
lights left on. The thing that amazed all present was
the reaction of the senior Officers; not one turned a
hair. The only deductions to be made were that either
their pensions were so secure that nothing need
worry them, or that their reputations were so far
gone anyway that one more dubious event was of no
importance.

There is no sure way to judge the success of a dinner
party. You should certainly pay no attention to the
comments in subsequent bread-and-butter letters;
the only thing you can guarantee about those is that

the author feels duty bound to turn the page before
she signs her name. She is thus forced to write gushy
adjectives at every opportunity to fill up the space.
One of the real hall marks of success is when one of
your guests has to leave and the others don't
stampede to the door with them. If the guests are still
with you at 2.00 a.m. things may have gone pretty
well but it is more likely to be an indication of how
free flowing the alcohol is. If your guests are with you
beyond this time it probably means that they are too
drunk or too tired to leave. Don't worry, they will go
soon enough in the morning when they are
discovered by your small children.

OUTWARD APPEARANCES

ROSE BY ANY OTHER NAME

Names in the Army are of vital importance. If you were born into it Mummy would have made sure that you were labelled correctly. The trouble with the Army is that names are public property and if yours isn't quite right, everyone knows. You appear on a document called the Staff List along with all the other wives. The Staff List contains such vital pieces of information as the full names of all the Officers, their addresses, phone numbers both at home and at work and the names of their wives and children. Thus, if there is a Wayne or Kylie lurking in a family, the truth will come out.

You can tell real Officers' wives because they may have been christened Virginia or Letitia, but they now prefer to be known by their nick-name. Animals and wild-life seem fairly popular, Panda, Mouse, Poppy, Bunny to name but a few. Really top-drawer wives can dare to get away with ones like Doodles and Yo-yo. You should only allow pet names like these to appear on the Staff List if at least one relative is a General and you are sure of your position in the pecking order. If your husband is in a Corps don't even consider it.

However, despite the fact that you cannot change your name, you can give your children a flying start by getting their names right. It is true that names go in fashions but there is nothing wrong in following trends, provided they are the right ones. Read the births columns of the Times if you are not sure what to pick. You can usually rely on it to give you some useful ideas. Boys names hardly seem to change, Charles, Alexander, James, Andrew and now Harry (what a surprise) populate Officers' patches worldwide. Girls are more tricky with Charlotte, Abigail and Elizabeth being replaced by Rose, Holly, Olivia, Flora, and the like. There are some perennials like Alice and Victoria, but never Vicky. Whatever you do, don't try to be original. Like all things in the Army, if you conform you can't be wrong.

Conforming does have its drawbacks though, go to the door and call your children in for their tea and six other Victorias and Harrys will appear too.

DRESS

Now that you have picked the right sort of name to be known by, it is vitally important that you look the part too. You may have already noticed that 'dress' has already featured largely in this book. This is because its role in the life of an Army wife is so great.

You will have also noticed that Officers' wives simply adore uniforms. It's absolutely true that there's nothing like a man in uniform. Young Officers look as perfect in their uniforms as a tray of graded eggs (and they get smashed just as easily too). While uniform is undeniably neat and tidy it often covers a multitude of sins, like underwear which has been on since the last exercise and shirts with so many tram lines you could run an entire transport network on them. So if you don't investigate what is under the surface before you get married you may get a nasty shock.

It should therefore come as no surprise that Officers' wives want their own uniform too. Most wives have spent their lives before marriage in one. They went to the sort of school that was proud of its uniform. You know, the sort that have uniform knickers. They were probably dressed in bottle green or navy – they continue to be favourite colours. Then quite a lot of wives were nurses or in the Army themselves, and those that weren't, were nannies or teachers. In, or surrounded by uniform throughout her youth and early twenties, an average Army wife can't cope with non-conformity, and, hardest of all, a decision first thing in the morning. Whatever else one may wish to say about uniform, it does make getting dressed an absolute cinch.

'ONE'S MIND GOES BLANK THINKING WHAT TO WEAR'

Casual observers of Army wives and in particular, Officers' wives, may be forgiven for thinking that they have drawn their outfits from some Army store. This alas is not true and Army wives must buy their own uniforms. In the absence of Dress Regulations from the Ministry of Defence itself wives have been forced to develop their own uniform; how popular it has proved to be. No matter which patch you live on, or where in the world it is, or which Regiment your husband calls his own, the wives will all be dressed alike. The standard dress allows for differences in husbands' ranks to be made clear. Whether you are out shopping, at a coffee morning or just browsing in the Thrift Shop, it's always most useful to know who's who.

DRESS IN THE PAST

Ten years ago the day wear for an Officer's wife was much less flattering than today. Then, she was stuck with sensible shoes, thick tights, a tweed skirt, twin-set and pearls. Her husband's rank was denoted by the quality of the tweed and the size of the pearls. Wives looked comfortable, homely and Establishment, even if their skirts bagged and sagged. Presumably their appearance was the origin of the term 'old bag'. You can sometimes catch a glimpse of this past era when retired Officers' wives come to wives lunches and coffee mornings. They are usually someone's mother-in-law and should be avoided unless you feel like switching off and nodding rhythmically to a monologue of life in their day.

The tweedy look was highly suitable for walking the dogs on Salisbury Plain, attending horse shows,

'AN OLD BAG'

Christmas bazzars and coffee mornings, all of which
were (and still are) part of a wife's daily routine. With
rationing within living memory, it made sense to
have one outfit that covered all occasions, and all
figures. A-line tweedy skirts could be dreadfully
unflattering, and were guaranteed to make every
wife wish at least one bulge away, if not two or three.
They were hardest on the wives with a 'fuller' figure.
(Since most of them were married to senior Officers
one had better not call them fat.) However, body fat,
thick tights and tweed were essential to stop
hypothermia setting in whilst watching

interminable parades in freezing weather and
spending every weekend on the touch line,
supporting the Regiment. Forced to do that anyone
would welcome a bit of insulation.

DRESS TODAY

The new uniform is much softer and looks good on
most shapes and sizes. Some things have been kept on
from the old style, pearls being one of the more
noticeable items. There is also a winter and a
summer uniform now; this is a very popular
innovation because husbands also go into summer
order and it's nice to have things in common isn't it?
In summer, you should sport a Liberty print skirt,
Laura Ashley frilly blouse and a black velvet
hairband or bow. Real Officers' wives wear their hair
swept back off their face. They have either led such a
stress free life that their foreheads are as smooth as
the skin of a fresh peach or they are senior enough not
to care. Hairbows are useful for improving your back
view and everyone will certainly know that you are
an Officer's wife. However, if your back view is your
best asset it does make it difficult to engage in
conversation with the right amount of poise.

   In the winter you swop the skirt for a grey or navy
flannel one with a navy lambswool or cashmere
sweater. It goes without saying that buying poor
quality clothes is a false economy. As they are all you
will be wearing for the next twenty years or so it
really pays to buy them to last. A pearl necklace looks
good throughout the year. Some Officers' wives from
good families will have no doubt inherited their
pearls. But if they are not in your trousseau when you

'SHE MUST BE A BRIGADIER'S WIFE, SHE'S GOT FIVE ROWS OF PEARLS'

get married, you will need to do some serious
shopping on your honeymoon. Pearls are the badges
of rank in a wife's uniform. It's simple really, one row
of pearls for Captains , two for Majors and three for
Colonels. You will find that Brigadiers' wives and
above wear other badges of rank like jewel encrusted
Regimental and Corps brooches or even pearled
headbands.

A word on tights. Navy, red or green by all means,
but never flesh coloured. Many wives pick a colour to
match their sweater. Athough it is worth
remembering that red tights can cause a bit of a stir
in older company who mix up the saying 'Red hat no
knickers' with 'red tights no knickers'. But if current
fashions in skirt lengths stay as they are, there'll be
little chance that you will display an indiscreet knee,
let alone anything else. Patterned tights are
becoming more popular. It is advisable to steer well
clear of the ones patterned in the Union Jack, little
pigs or abstract swirls. One wife got very confused
when the Medical Officer kept inquiring after her
health and suggesting that she ought to go and see
him. Eventually she did. It was only when she had
her tights round her ankles that he realised that she
hadn't got varicose veins after all. She is still trying
to work out if she misunderstood his intentions.

Accessories are important if an Officer's wife is to
keep her appearance up to scratch. If you must go
shopping with a carrier bag at least make sure it's
from Harrods or Dickens and Jones and not
Sainsburys. It is far better to invest in a small wicker
basket. Real Officers' wives carry them on their arm
or over the handle bars of a bicycle. How it is done
totally baffles me, but real Officers' wives can get the
entire week's shopping for a family of five, two dogs
and a cat into one wicker basket. Where most people

use the seat in the supermarket trolley for a
screaming child, they use it for the dear little basket
they couldn't be without anywhere.

Always useful, and an absolute 'must' in a real
Officer's wife's wardrobe is a head scarf. In previous
generations this was worn on the head with the knot
tied firmly on the chin. This was most important, and
almost impossible unless you had been bred like the
Royal Family to have the right shape of chin, or
better still, no chin at all. As only peasants tie their
headscarves under the chin this is a sure-fire way of
checking out your credentials. Of course it was and
still is pretty vital that you make sure you only wear
Hermes scarves. You might as well chuck everything
else out. Every senior wife has trained her eagle eyes
to scan your dress across a parade ground for the
minutest of details. Wearing a Hermes scarf lets you
into that elite club of Officers' wives whose husbands
don't balk at paying outrageous prices. It is after all a
sign of affluence. In today's times where the general
rule is 'if you've got it, flaunt it' Officers' wives now
have a passion for wearing their Hermes scarves
draped across the shoulders of their most battered
Barbour or best cashmere coat alike.

On marrying an Army Officer you may well think
that you can get away with wearing something
different. Be Warned! Within five years of joining the
system your wardrobe will be the same as everyone
else's. And however much you try to kid yourself that
you 'have only got the Barbour because it is so
practical when one is forced to stand around in the
rain', in your heart of hearts you know that you have
found it easier to conform rather than keep fighting
the system. Turn up wearing the wrong kit to a
function and you will feel more uncomfortable than
Lady Godiva did without a saddle. Many people

pooh-pooh the idea that Officers' wives wear a
uniform. But you can be sure that if you go to such an
occasion as the Camberley Horse Show the vast
majority of those present will be wearing a grey
flannel skirt, navy blue sweater, a frilly blouse
topped by a Barbour jacket, head scarf and, if wet,
green Hunter wellies.

JUST A BIT OF A DO

Army wives hate not knowing exactly what to wear
to a social occasion. For the functions that matter
instructions are given on the invitation. How very
sensible you might think. However, the instructions
are only for the men. Wives are often regarded as
being decorative and are allowed to wear what they
like... within certain limits of course. More
experienced wives know what to wear with 'Mess
Kit', 'Black Tie', 'Lounge Suits' and 'Planters' for
example. The best advice I can give is that you should
ask the opinion of other wives if you are not
absolutely certain. Unless you are very sure of what
is de rigueur its best not to let your outfit be a
surprise. Most inexperienced wives tend to be
underdressed for social occasions mistakenly
believing they are going out to relax and enjoy
themselves.

The general rule is that flesh should be covered up.
(In most cases it looks better that way.) The rule used
to be that your shoulders had to be covered up at the
table during dinner. Although no such rules exist
about the length of your dress it is generally
considered risky to show your knees, let alone
anything else. Nowadays things are becoming a bit

more relaxed, but you should not go too far. Just remember the angle of view that Mess waiters have when they are serving you. If the poor man's hand starts shaking and he drops your food because he can see all the way down to your navel, you only have yourself to blame.

'HOW TO LOOK A REAL TIT AT A DINNER NIGHT'

Putting 'Black Tie' on an invitation confuses a lot of wives. The agonising decision to wear long or short may go on for days, and to their husband's dismay, be the subject of interminable phone calls. Most wives dread being the odd one out. Once you get to be quite senior it doesn't matter a damn what you wear. The other wives will assume that they misread the invitation. Rank does have its privileges. So too does poise. On one dinner night I went to, the Ladies retired to the Ladies room after the speeches. After applying more lipstick and having a good gossip we joined the men at the bar. No one noticed that one of the wives had her dress tucked in her knickers. When her husband told her, she exclaimed in a loud voice 'God, it's hot in here' and ordered another glass of champagne. She certainly had the makings of a real Officer's wife.

A young wife will probably want to wear a stunning evening dress to a Mess dinner. Do remember though that in a Regiment serving overseas you may have to attend half a dozen or so in the course of a posting. If you wear anything too amazing, you may succeed in making the other wives sick with envy, but they will all remark if it ever reappears out of your wardrobe for a second airing. Wear something unmemorable and you can have it in and out of the cupboard like a yo-yo. You have to be most careful if your husband is a member of a Regiment rather than a Corps. In a Regiment you will get stuck with the same people for most of your adult life. With the latter, he gets 'trickle' posted. This means that he moves on at a different time to all the other Officers – people are arriving and departing all the time. This is a wonderful thing because you can rotate the contents of your wardrobe every two years and parade all the old stuff in front of a new audience. Wonderful for saving money.

HOBBY HORSES

To be the Complete Army Wife all you need to be able to do is ski and ride. Which is easy if you know how. Real Officers and their wives could probably do both of these before they could walk and most certainly before they went to school. The Army suits them to a 'T'. It not only provides postings to Germany so they can get to the slopes almost every weekend in the winter but it also lets them have stabling for their horses at a knock-down price.

But what should you do if you can't ride and have about as much chance of balancing on skis as a drunk on a tight-rope? The solution to the first problem is simple, unless of course you are terrified of horses. You must get involved with Riding for the Disabled. This does not mean that you have to shoot yourself in the foot in order to qualify; far from it, the more able-bodied the better. It gives you a fighting chance of being able to skip out of the way when one of the horses is careless about where it is putting its feet. Anyway, helping out with this once a week or so will have a two-fold pay-off. Firstly, you will be doing something worthwhile and secondly you will be mixing with all the right people. Get in with the horsey-set and you can't go far wrong. You may even get invited to their dinner parties and your husband's promotion chances are bound to prosper. And if you play your cards right no-one need ever know that you can't actually ride yourself.

Skiing is a bit more tricky. I mean it's a bit pointless going on a skiing holiday if neither of you can ski. This leaves you with three options. Either you get yourselves posted to UK where the pressure is off somewhat, or you start having children. Failing that you just have to bite the bullet and learn. Lots of people do manage to learn when their teens are a distant memory but it is a lot harder. And hardest of all is learning to keep your temper when the local school children invade the ski lift and show off their abilities right in your path causing you to fall over. All done deliberately but you must not rise to the bait. Just grit your teeth and think of King Herod.

For both pastimes the right kit is essential. Turn up to the stables without your green Hunter wellies on and you will be docked ten brownie points instantly. Ray-Ban sunglasses on the ski slopes are a must together with this year's ski fashions. Posing is very important so you must be able to do it with style. This is especially so in the German Alps where a three month ski exercise called Snow Queen is held annually. Senior Officers like to visit their troops on this exercise and invariably their wives go too, so you never know who you may meet. Make sure you are prepared.

If you can't face skiing or riding then you could try clay pigeon shooting or sailing. Wind surfing is very popular with the junior set because it gives yet more opportunities for the poseur. It's a shame that a roof rack has not yet been invented that will take both skis and a wind surfer....

If your pursuits are more arty, then on no account should you boast about your skills. If you do you will become lemonned for all sorts of unenviable jobs. Drop a whisper that you can paint and guess who will find herself painting all the sets for the Garrison

'THE PERFECT POSEUR'

Panto? Mention that you once made a skirt, or worse still, that you own a sewing machine, and you'll be running up costumes for the entire cast. Admit to owning a word processor and there you are, running the wives' magazine.

Lastly, don't try and compete with your husband. He will get most upset if you take up jogging or target shooting or something equally sporty. He will be scared that you may end up beating him. If you want to go swimming he will suggest that you might as well take the kids along too. Not quite what you had in mind. Being sporty is his territory, so don't encroach on it.

THE FLOWER CLUB

Without the flower club the Real Officer's wife is quite lost. Flower arranging is definitely an OK hobby for the promotion conscious wife. The flower club is the hub of the universe for real Officers' wives. Luckily, flower clubs are now so universal that she can be pretty sure of finding one wherever her husband happens to be posted. Should the system break down, she will soon remedy matters by starting one up; or if she is really senior, she will found one, and find someone else to do all the work.

The Mecca of all the flower clubs is to be found in Germany at Bielefeld. One does not attend to see, but to be seen. Flowers play second fiddle to the other attractions there. Firstly one can be sure of being able to check out any alterations to the ubiquitous uniform. If bows on shoes suddenly become spotted or striped, the first place these all important changes will be seen is at the flower club. Secondly, it is vastly popular and wives drive from all over West Germany to attend. It is therefore a hot bed of gossip, rumour, and exchange of news – if you are not there, you may find that you are the main topic of the conversation. Thirdly, you can be sure of picking up any number of little designer knick-knacks being flogged by other Officers' wives. Hand painted is the order of the day; arty wives will paint anything. So if you fancy a hand painted nursery chair, earrings, plant pot, or child's picture, this is the place to go. (It's just a hangover from National Service days when if it moved you saluted it, if it didn't, you painted it.)

Last, and seemingly least, come the flowers and the demonstration. This is usually done by someone extraordinarily talented who has been especially flown out from the UK for the occasion. You are then shown how to make the most of DM200 worth of flowers. Given that quantity of flowers, and the most wonderful selection of containers, most people could come up with a passable effort. Being only in possession of three vases and having a strictly limited budget when it comes to life's luxuries, one would rather know what to do with four tulips and a bunch of daffodils.

By now you will have guessed correctly that you should 'Dress' for the flower club. It is not considered good form to roll up in jeans and a sweater. Smart cotton frocks with coloured tights and patent pumps in the summer or a suit in the winter are the minimum standard. Unlike the Royal Enclosure at Ascot, you will not be refused entry, you'll just wish you had been.

After the demonstrator has finished, the arrangements are raffled. This is fine if you happen to win something quite manageable, but how do you transport a giant pedestal arrangement across half of Germany on a hot day, in a 2CV with three other wives in it?

CROSS COUNTRY DANCING

Depending on your husband's Regiment you may or may not have to take up country dancing. The country in question is Scotland, so if your idea of reeling is getting plastered you will do better to keep clear of it. However if your husband is in a Scottish Regiment there will be little chance of avoiding it. Real Officers and their wives take up the sport early on in life and are well versed in how to 'strip the willow' and 'set to their partner'. He learns how to do it at Sandhurst where the authorities bus in lots of suitable girls from the local finishing schools as live bait. This encourages some of the cadets to turn up to the weekly class. She learns how to do it as it's considered essential knowledge before you come out. If you come to it late on in life you will find it not only complicated but exhausting. You may have been told that a good bonk is the equivalent of a three mile run,

but you will now find out that an evening of Scottish
Country Dancing is the same as the London
Marathon. But look on the bright side, you needn't
bother with aerobics anymore.

'CROSS COUNTRY DANCING'

WHAT'S FREE TIME?

SEND THEM AWAY

Make no mistake, your children will have to go away to boarding school. Whatever your views on private education, however strong your feelings against boarding schools, before long you will find yourself labelling trunks and tuck boxes. If you have had the luxury of a childhood in one place and an education at the local grammar school your views on this subject are easy to understand. Real Officers' wives don't have these problems; they have been dragged from pillar to post and saw boarding school as an oasis of stability in an otherwise turbulent world. After your twelfth move you too will start to change your mind about education.

You will discover that your darling little treasures which you have nurtured so carefully, begin to show signs of getting muddled with their maths and reading schemes. Not so very surprising if they have already been at four schools and they aren't quite six. Some children, like my daughter, take a while to settle into a new school and make no progress at all for six months. Consequently, by the time she's learnt the name of her teacher and those of her classmates it's time to move again. She may only be able to read the first six letters of the alphabet but she is brilliant at remembering names and faces. This will be very useful to her if she too marries into the Army.

You will hear most mothers of young children dreading the prospect of sending the little darlings away. Even if you are not against boarding schools the wrench is still great. Of course, there are exceptions. Some mothers send their children away at five so they can get on with an illicit affair, or find sufficient time to really work on their husband's promotion prospects. The most common age for sending them away is eight or nine. Boys are sometimes sent younger in the belief that they need more discipline at an earlier age. Army Officers may be able to train their gun dogs, get Regiments to leap to attention at one word of command but children totally defeat them. Therefore there is a need for schools to fill the gap. That this is necessary may seem somewhat surprising when you consider the organisation which employs their fathers depends upon discipline. But then, you have only to observe the young Officers when they're drunk at a dinner night to realise that discipline is something that comes from outside rather than within.

Having taken the plunge and exiled the little mites to a suitable school parents quickly seem to adjust to the loss. Mothers who seemed inconsolable at their departure rarely seem to mind when little Harry is only allowed home once a term. Indeed the reason for choosing a boarding school sometimes seems to be that it only allows the children out infrequently. The excuse being that the children get fed up with being left in at weekends if their parents are posted abroad. More likely so that the parents can plan their shopping trips to Paris or improve their golf. Some parents are very sensible about sending their children away and begin by sending them to board weekly at a nearby school while they are in England. This may seem as crazy as a woman wearing maternity clothes when all she has done is stopped taking the Pill, but it does mean the children get used to the idea. It also gives the parents a chance to reacquaint themselves with such things as lie-ins, conversation and each other.

The most common complaint you are likely to hear about boarding school (apart from the fees that is) is about the length of the holidays. Around Christmas and Easter you are likely to hear such comments as 'I'm sorry, I can't make lunch on Tuesday; the kids are home. They're off for a bloody month this time.' Mothers long for their offspring to come home, and then long for them to go away again. Which all goes to prove how things don't change. When they were toddlers and asleep in their cots at night you might be forgiven for wishing you could eat them up. But in the morning when they were awake, by God, you wish you had.

If you were born to being an Officer's wife choosing a school is a breeze. Your daughters go to your old school and your sons go to his. You don't have to worry too much about putting names down and the like. After all, isn't that the whole point about the Old Boy network? If you didn't like your old school and want to try something different you will have loads of friends who will be able to recommend a long list of suitable ones so you will have ample choice. You should certainly avoid some of these new fangled mixed schools. But beware, times are changing and I've even heard rumours of girls at Eton and Harrow.

If you don't have this sort of background then you are going to find choosing a school an exhausting business. It's rather like choosing a continental holiday. After hours of debate and reading through piles of brochures you finally make your choice, only to find out that you can't be offered a place for the next three years.

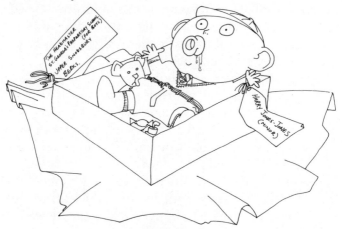

'MAKING SURE OF A PLACE'

The best thing to do is to make a list of schools near the grannies (to help out with half term and exeats) and then visit them. Don't fall into the trap of taking the children with you in the mistaken belief that they can choose which one they like. Present them with any kind of choice and they'll have you traipsing from one to the other and back again. They will finally announce that they can't remember which one it was that they did like and that they don't want to go away to school anyway. This makes you feel guilty about the whole thing and you put off the decision for another month or two.

EXTRA-CURRICULAR ACTIVITIES

Now that you have your children safely ensconced in a good school you will find that extra-curricular activities loom large on the agenda. I am not talking about all those 'extras' on offer at the school like ballet, riding, elocution and music, all of which will help bump up the bill to something resembling the National Debt. No, these are things for you to do and you will find the emphasis is on the word 'extra', as in 'more than you bargained for'. In fact I am talking about committees.

When Officers' wives aren't at coffee mornings, this is where you will find them. Just like in the good old House of Commons, most of the real work gets done in committees. Ostensibly committees are formed to decide things. You'll hear wives who can't decide anything for themselves say in a loud voice at coffee mornings and other gatherings 'Let's form a committee. We'll need a chairwoman, a secretary and a treasurer at least.' Before you know it the organisation of the Garrison Children's Christmas Party Committee is more important than the party itself. But be careful not to express an opinion about this, if you do you will be roped in too.

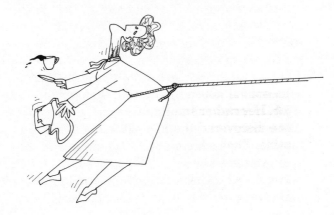

'GETTING ROPED IN'

There are some Officers' wives who love to organise things and run committees. They've usually succeeded in organising their husband and children who no longer offer any challenge. If you are lucky enough to be posted with wives who are like this, the best thing to do is to leave them to it. They'll resent any interference. Of course they'll complain to their friends that they're always left to do everything and that no one ever gives them any support. This grumbling is one of the perks of being a committee organiser. These dedicated organisers will form committees to decide upon the format of an all purpose committee if they find themselves devoid of any other sort of organising.

You may be really unfortunate and get posted with a senior Officer's wife who hates committees; or worse still, your husband gets promoted and you find yourself expected to run them. In which case, be prepared for some hard times ahead. If you are not careful you will find yourself organising the Wives Club Christmas disco, the NAAFI customer relations committee and taking the chair of the library committee. Consider the case of a friend of mine. She was delighted when her husband was promoted – all her hard work at dinner parties had clearly paid off. She was even more ecstatic when she moved into her enormous house in Germany, which went with the job. Her rather smug smile was soon wiped out when she discovered the pile of files on the dining room table. They each contained the details of the committees she was on. There was one for SSAFA, the NAAFI, the Mess, the Wives' Club, the Thrift Shop and at least two more. One for each day of the week.

So you can see that it is essential to get your children away before you reach the dizzy heights of being a Major's wife. Otherwise you won't be able to fully assume the role that the Army has mapped out for you.

THE THRIFT SHOP

You will find that even if you manage to dodge all the committees, you are bound to find yourself helping out in the Thrift Shop. To those of you who have not yet come across one of these shops, they are places where Officers' wives go to buy the Soldiers' wives' old clothes.

If anyone was to suggest that an Officer's wife would like to wear clothes cast off by one of the Soldier's wives, there would be an outcry. However, put the same clothes into the Thrift Shop and they are transformed into 'bargains'. In this new guise it is all quite acceptable.

The shop is run by Officer's wives so that they get first pick of all the stuff that comes in to be sold. In this way they can ensure that little James and Camilla only get to wear the best quality second hand clothes. Baby clothes and prams are always particularly good value.

One could suggest that Officers' wives are mean with their money as most of their children are kitted out entirely from this source. In order to convince themselves to the contrary a percentage of the takings goes to charity. Consciences thus assuaged, the whole set up is good for morale all round. Apart from being a nice little earner for the Soldiers' wives it gives them no end of a laugh to see their old clothes being paraded around the Garrison by the Colonel's children. Furthermore, Officers' wives can congratulate themselves on their bargain hunting. (Very necessary when little Emily's child benefit is being blown on the black labrador's quarantine.)

THE FINAL POLISH

ATTENTION TO DETAIL

People in the Army are forever saying, 'It's not what you know, but who you know that counts'. Which is true if you instinctively know all the 'whats'. If you don't, those little bits of missing information and social graces will let you down so badly. If you've got the pearls, the dog, the headscarf and the nanny you should be practically fire-proof as an Officer's wife. But your background will show like an overlong petticoat if you have a preference for bitter and vote Labour.

The trouble is, you can come unstuck in so many different little ways. Take dinner party invitations for example. One would think that once one had RSVPed, dined and finally written the bread and butter letter it would be quite in order to throw the card out. Not the correct procedure at all. They should be put on the mantlepiece, or failing that, the television as a reminder of a debt that you owe. It's similar to getting a red bill from the Gas Board (only people tend to hide those away rather than display them). In this instance, the more you have ranged around the place the higher your social status – it all goes to prove how enormously popular you are. However, it does mean that you have debts to repay. You will see harassed Officers' wives going around saying, 'We owe hundreds of people. Perhaps we could clear the lot up with a drinks do?' They have every right to look harassed; a final demand may come their way in the form of 'If we don't hear from you soon, we'll be on your doorstep for dinner on Friday'.

It's probably worth mentioning a word of warning about newspapers, magazines and so on. You can come unstuck quite drastically by having the wrong newspapers and magazines delivered. It is absolutely essential to be able to scatter the correct selection of periodicals over your coffee table, especially if you are expecting a visit from the Commanding Officer's wife. Take care to remove the jam splodges first in case she decides to pick one up. She will not be impressed if she has to engage in a wrestling match in order to unstick it. You will score very highly if you have a current copy of 'The Lady' and 'Homes and Gardens' but equally you can be marked down as a 'no hoper' if you are a reader of the 'Mirror' or worse still the 'Guardian'. Most Officer's wives, and their husbands too for that matter, read the 'Telegraph'. Apart from having a good crossword and a Court and Social page (so you can check up on what your chums are up to) it has sound Tory values. It won't contaminate your brain with any thoughts of equal rights or other namby-pamby trendy nonsense.

Whilst on the subject of politics I should just like to offer a few words of advice. Officially politics don't exist in the Army, or any of the other Services for that matter. Like women and religion, discussion about politics is barred from dinner tables throughout the world. (That's why Army Officers are always talking about themselves. With the three most interesting subjects banned from the conversation people have to resort to the fourth most interesting one.) However, it's probably a good thing that Officers and their wives don't discuss politics. For a start there is usually not much to say – they all support the Tories. Their only concern is that the Tories are getting far too soft and left wing.

Occasionally and rather accidentally there are Officers and their wives who show some sympathy with socialist ideals. They will have long since been labelled as 'Pinkos' and should they open their mouths they will get shouted down by everyone else.

In practice, politics are pretty irrelevant. Moving so often, by the time your name is on the Electoral Register you have long been gone. Besides which, in most places you don't live there long enough even to find out the name of the local candidate, let alone which party he or she belongs to.

HOUSEWORK

The state of your house is all part of your image. Everything else may be gaining you full marks but you can drop lots of bonus points by having a house that looks like a Liverpudlian rubbish tip. The only reason that your house should measure up is so that it looks as though you employ a cleaner. It is unlikely that on your husband's pay, and with the mounting cost of all those dinner parties that you will be able to afford one, so you must keep things up to scratch yourself. If, because of committees, Riding for the Disabled, walking the dogs and so forth you find this impossible, then invite the really important people around in the evening. If you spray furniture polish around like air freshener and use candles as the only light source, you will probably find that they don't notice the fluff, in balls like tumbleweed, rolling around the carpet. Should one of your visitors lose something under a chair or down the side of the sofa, in the gloom, don't let them ferret under the cushions themselves. Your image will be ruined if they drag out, not only their handbag or whatever, but also a mouldy apple core, a pair of socks, a half eaten biscuit and a dirty hanky.

JARGON

This is not something that real Officers' wives use in their day to day speech, but it is important to have a working knowledge of it so you don't lose your dignity and look a complete berk through lack of understanding. Sam Browne, for example is not a friend of your husband's. A Camp Follower is what you now are, not a poofter hanging around the barracks. Likewise, hors de combat are not prostitutes within the Garrison area. If someone tells you to pull up a sandbag don't wander round the Mess trying to find one. The chances are that you will only be asked to do this if someone is going to Swing the Lamp – jargon for 'boring the pants off every one with When I Was There stories'.

LOOS

The last word of advice I can give to any Officer's wife is that she throws away the crinoline doll hiding the spare loo roll. It may have been a wedding present from a favourite aunt, but it is destined to scupper your chances in the Army game. If you must decorate your loo with anything other than the brush, try

'HORS DE COMBAT'

breaking away from the group photographs and show a bit of originality. To give the illusion of class, especially if your husband hasn't been photographed in the presence of Royalty, try leaving a load of shooting sticks lying around and a couple of deer stalkers. It is also advisable to put a large bowl of pot-pourri on the window sill as the Army has never been known to provide an extractor fan. The best loos that I have visited have antique plates covering the walls and a profusion of silk flowers in the window. The soap is of the highest quality from Yves Saint Laurent and there is no trace of a potty or a slimy flannel. The towels, naturally, are monogrammed, expensive and clean.

When your husband is over the rank of Captain, you may find sufficient space for a magazine rack or even a bookcase. These should be stuffed with books of the adult humour variety. You may have noticed that these are usually in dreadfully bad taste and designed exclusively for men. Books like 'The Bad Taste Book of Warfare' or 'Up the Falklands' have little feminine appeal. When the loo is your only refuge from your family, isn't it disheartening to discover there is nothing for you to read when you have locked the door? At least you've now got something to redress the balance.